VOLUME SIX
Allied Fighters: Bell P-39 & P-400 Airacobra
South & Southwest Pacific 1942–1944

MICHAEL JOHN CLARINGBOULD

Avonmore Books

Pacific Profiles Volume Six

Allied Fighters: Bell P-39 & P-400 Airacobra
South & Southwest Pacific 1942–1944

Michael John Claringbould

ISBN: 978-0-6452469-0-2

First published 2022 by Avonmore Books

Avonmore Books
PO Box 217
Kent Town
South Australia 5071
Australia

Phone: (61 8) 8431 9780
avonmorebooks.com.au

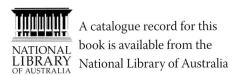
Cover design & layout by Diane Bricknell

Cover artwork captions
Front Cover: A selection of profiles (top to bottom) are a P-400 from the "Pair-a-Dice" flight of the 67th FS (Profile 46), P-39K-1 Lilly of the 12th FS (Profile 3), one of the many versions of P-400 BX163 during its 1942 Port Moresby career and P-39Q-5 Little Sir Echo, named by Captain Lyndall Tate of the 82nd RS(F).

Back Cover: P-39Q The Dorothy D serial 42-19973 of the 82nd RS(F) totes a 1,000-pound bomb towards a target on New Guinea's northern coast in May 1944.

Contents

The author (centre) with villagers at Kosipe village in the Papua New Guinea highlands in 2014 before departing to locate wreckage of P-39N 42-19041 operated by the 110th RS (F) which went MIA on 20 January 1944 in bad weather and crashed into nearby mountains. The guitarist, seated alongside the author, is Mark Leilei from the Papua New Guinea National Museum & Art Gallery.

About the Author

Michael Claringbould – Author & Illustrator

Michael spent his formative years in Papua New Guinea in the 1960s, during which he became fascinated by the many WWII aircraft wrecks which lay around the country and also throughout the Solomon Islands. Michael subsequently served widely overseas as an Australian diplomat throughout Southeast Asia and the Pacific, including Fiji (1995-1998) and Papua New Guinea (2003-2005). Michael has authored and illustrated numerous books on Pacific War aviation. His history of the Tainan Naval Air Group in New Guinea, *Eagles of the Southern Sky*, received worldwide acclaim as the first English-language history of a Japanese fighter unit, and was subsequently translated into Japanese. An executive member of Pacific Air War History Associates, Michael holds a pilot license and PG4 paraglider rating. He continues to develop his skills as a digital aviation artist and cartoonist.

Other Books by the Author

Black Sunday (2000)

Eagles of the Southern Sky (2012, with Luca Ruffato)

F4U Corsair versus A6M2/3/4 Zero-sen, Solomons and Rabaul 1943-44 (Osprey, 2022)

Nemoto's Travels The illustrated saga of a Japanese floatplane pilot in the first year of the Pacific War (2021)

Operation I-Go Yamamoto's Last Offensive – New Guinea and the Solomons April 1943 (2020)

P-39 / P-400 Airacobra versus A6M2/3 Zero-sen New Guinea 1942 (Osprey, 2018)

P-47D Thunderbolt versus Ki-43 Hayabusa New Guinea 1943/44 (Osprey, 2020)

Pacific Adversaries Volume One Japanese Army Air Force vs The Allies New Guinea 1942-1944 (2019)

Pacific Adversaries Volume Two Imperial Japanese Navy vs The Allies New Guinea & the Solomons 1942-1944 (2020)

Pacific Adversaries Volume Three Imperial Japanese Navy vs The Allies New Guinea & the Solomons 1942-1944 (2020)

Pacific Adversaries Volume Four Imperial Japanese Navy vs The Allies - The Solomons 1943-1944 (2021)

Pacific Profiles Volume One Japanese Army Fighters New Guinea & the Solomons 1942-1944 (2020)

Pacific Profiles Volume Two Japanese Army Bomber & Other Units, New Guinea and the Solomons 1942-44 (2020)

Pacific Profiles Volume Three Allied Medium Bombers, A20 Series, South West Pacific 1942-44 (2020)

Pacific Profiles Volume Four Allied Fighters: Vought F4U Corsair Series Solomons Theatre 1943-1944 (2021)

Pacific Profiles Volume Five Japanese Navy Zero Fighters (land-based) New Guinea and the Solomons 1942-1944 (2021)

Pacific Profiles Volume Six Allied Fighters: Bell P-39 & P-400 Airacobra South & Southwest Pacific 1942-1944 (2022)

Pacific Profiles Volume Seven Allied Transports: Douglas C-47 series South & Southwest Pacific 1942-1945 (2022)

South Pacific Air War Volume 1: The Fall of Rabaul December 1941–March 1942 (2017, with Peter Ingman)

South Pacific Air War Volume 2: The Struggle for Moresby March–April 1942 (2018, with Peter Ingman)

South Pacific Air War Volume 3: Coral Sea & Aftermath May-June 1942 (2019, with Peter Ingman)

South Pacific Air War Volume 4: Buna & Milne Bay June-September 1942 (2020, with Peter Ingman)

South Pacific Air War Volume 5: Crisis in Papua September – December 1942 (2022, with Peter Ingman)

Introduction

The intent of this book is to unravel the confusion of Pacific Airacobra markings which has contributed to the creation of a suite of fictitious aircraft which unfortunately continue to exist in art, model aircraft boxes, history publications and colourised photos.

Bell's unique Airacobra was produced for three years from 1941 until 1944. American pilots lent it several unkind nicknames, including "Iron Dog". Whilst much has been written about the type, lazy scholarship has caused confusion and inaccuracy about its Pacific markings. This volume corrects these past markings inaccuracies and presents many new profiles for the first time. It also explains the numerous markings systems and how exchange between units created a system of hybrid schemes.

Shortly after the 35th and 36th Fighter Squadrons opened the Airacobra New Guinea air war in April 1942, another three Airacobra squadrons from the 35th Pursuit Group which arrived in Australia in late February 1942 were exclusively equipped with P-400s. As the units moved around, were rotated through combat, or needed repairs these airframes were liberally traded between units. This situation led to a labyrinth of complex and interwoven unit markings. This was exacerbated by an accelerated rotation of units from June 1942 onwards, bolstered by the importation of more P-39Ds from August 1942. The mixing of inventories between six squadrons meant that many airframes carried multiple unit markings; *inter alia* mixtures of squadron numbers and alphabetical letters, shark's teeth and nose art. Combined with rudder replacements, painted repairs and some P-400s painted over with olive drab schemes, it is easy to understand why Airacobras from these units have been so misrepresented over the years.

Matters become more complex when it is underlined that it is a myth that P-39s can be discerned visually from the P-400 by the number of exhaust stubs – 12 stubs for the P-400 and six for the P-39 – along with whether the airframe has a 20mm (P-400) or 37mm (P-39) cannon mounted in the nose. The initial batch of P-39D-1s was powered by the export E4 model of the 12-cylinder V-1710 Allison – the same engine installed in the P-400 – equipped with a dozen exhaust stubs. Then the P-39F had an electric pitch control propeller and the same dozen exhaust subs. Whilst all P-400s had the 20mm cannon and later model P-39Ds the 37mm version, several batches of P-39D-1s and P-39F defy the trend and were equipped with the 20mm cannon.

However, another key point particularly poignant to Pacific Airacobras is that all Allison engines and cannon types were readily interchangeable in the field. Pilots considered the 37mm M4 cannon to be ineffective due to its curved trajectory and slow rate of fire. It is not surprising that pilots showed a strong preference for the 20mm cannon and hence the slow firing 37mm weapon was replaced at the first opportunity.

The only certain way to identify a P-400, aside from its two-tone camouflage scheme, is by the presence of a tubular strut reinforcement attached to the top of the canopy, a detail rarely detectable in wartime photographs. Whilst P-400s sported the unique RAF Dark Green and

Dark Earth camouflage over Duck Egg Blue applied in the factory, exposure to harsh tropical conditions often blurred this unique paint scheme in black and white photos. Furthermore, some P-400s were painted olive drab in the field before reassignment or following repairs. Finally, some batches of later P-39D-1s initially ordered as P-400s were reissued to the USAAF in olive drab from the factory.

A curiosity is that six P-39Cs also found their way to Australia, some of which were assigned to the 35th Air Depot at Townsville. Others found their way into RAAF service, but it appears that only one (40-2995) found its way into combat, briefly, with the 36th FS.

P-400s in the Pacific

The deployment of the P-400 to the Pacific has a curious history. The British Purchasing Commission first ordered Model 14A Airacobras from Bell in April 1940 after accepting the manufacturer's positive performance figures for the XP-39 prototype. Officially termed the Caribou I by the RAF but rarely referred to as such, the Airacobra I was identical to the P-39D-1, featuring the V-1710-E4 engine, long-barreled 20mm M1 cannon and six 0.303-inch calibre machine guns. The first of these reached Great Britain in mid-1941 where they were flight tested at Duxford. In August, No. 601 Squadron replaced its Hurricane IICs with these Airacobra Is. The squadron quickly ascertained that the Airacobra's performance above 20,000 feet was poor, and that the fighter's speed was slower than claimed. Additional performance deficiencies saw the Airacobra withdrawn from RAF service. More than two hundred were diverted to the Soviet Union, and a similar consignment was redirected to the USAAF Eighth Air Force following its arrival in Britain in the summer of 1942. A further 179 Airacobra Is pending delivery to the RAF were reassigned to the USAAC following Pearl Harbor, which in turn were redirected to Australia and the Pacific.

On 28 January 1942 the first Airacobras arrived in the Pacific aboard the USS *President Monroe*. These P-39D airframes were unloaded at Suva then barged to Nausori as described in the history of the 70th FS. About three weeks later on 20 February the first RAF-rejected P-400 Airacobras arrived in Australia, unloaded from the SS *Mormacstar* at Melbourne's wharves. A later shipment of P-39Ds was unloaded from shipping crates in Brisbane, then trucked and assembled at Amberley airfield 31 miles southwest of the city.

After initial deployment in New Guinea, a collective of Fifth Air Force P-400s was overhauled from June to October 1942 and reassigned to the South Pacific Area via New Caledonia. These included British serials BW151, -154, -156, -157, -158, -159, -160, -162, -165, -167; and BX150, -151, -152, -154, -156, -157, -158, -159, -160, -161, -162. Several P-400 survivors operated in New Guinea well into mid-1943. The 36th FS continued to operate the P-400 the longest; AP335, -347, -355 and -357 were lost to operations as late as August 1943. The 39th FS kept a P-39D in its inventory until May 1943 for training purposes, long after their transition to P-38s, and in New Caledonia a former 67th FS P-400 was utilised as a liaison hack by a service squadron until mid-1944.

In the New Guinea theatre Airacobras regularly passed through, were operated by or were reassigned to other units via maintenance units such as the 27th Air Depot, 46th Service Group and 8th Service Group. At times a handful were also operated by 5th Fighter Command and the 5th Air Force Replacement Pool. The same type of assignments occurred in the Solomons with the Thirteenth Air Force, including with the 29th Service Group.

From late July 1943 onwards the later model P-39N and P-39Qs appeared in the Pacific performing escort, ground attack and patrol duties, however ultimately in the fighter role the Airacobra was surpassed hereon by a suite of more modern and powerful USAAF, United States Marine Corps and United States Navy fighters.

Japanese airpower in mainland New Guinea and the Solomons was withdrawn from around the end of February 1944. Four Airacobra squadrons took up the role of supporting ground operations via strafing, low-level bombing and dive-bombing attacks; the 82nd and 100th Reconnaissance Squadrons (Fighter) in New Guinea and the 68th and 70th FS in the Solomons. These pilots soon discovered that low-level attack flying was different to reconnaissance flying, as thick jungle concealed all but the most obvious targets. Their missions also involved dropping surrender leaflets and smoke target markers for Allied bombers. Targets in New Guinea extended along the northern coast, and aside from Wewak included areas around Madang, Alexishafen, Bogadjim, and Tadji itself. In the Solomons the squadrons based at Torokina on Bougainville ranged as far as the Rabaul area and New Ireland.

These ground attack squadrons operated N and Q model P-39s. The P-39Ns had armour plate behind the pilot in earlier models replaced by bullet-proof glass. The P-39Qs had their wing-mounted 0.30-inch calibre machine guns replaced with pod-mounted 0.50-inch calibre machine guns in packs attached to under-wing hard points. Many Airacobras in the New Guinea squadrons were equipped with K-24 and K-25 cameras mounted in the aft fuselage. All were equipped with a 37mm cannon fired through the propeller hub, manufactured by the Oldsmobile Auto Company. Although their slow rate of fire rendered them ineffective for air-to-air combat, they excelled in the ground attack role where pilots guided their trajectory with machine gun tracer fire. Bomb loads varied and were much experimented with. These ground attack missions, the last Airacobras ones flown in the Pacific and barely acknowledged by history, continued until mid-July 1944 from Torokina and until the end of September 1944 from Tadji.

Despite the widespread use of Airacobras in the South Pacific by a dozen USAAF squadrons, intriguingly only one pilot is recognised as an Airacobra ace: Lieutenant William Fiedler. Fielder achieved this status with the 68th FS at Guadalcanal in 1943. This remained a bone of contention with several Fifth Air Force Airacobra pilots who were awarded three or four kills from the busy 1942 period. During the early New Guinea campaign records were poorly maintained and some claims were not recognised. While the USAAF also flew P-39s in the Aleutian and the Mediterranean theatres, Fielder remains the only USAAF Airacobra ace.

Michael John Claringbould
August 2021

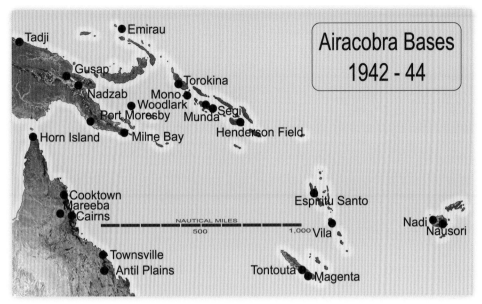

A map showing major Airacobra air bases in the South Pacific during 1942-1944. Some of these locations had several airfields, such as Port Moresby, Nadzab, Guadalcanal, Milne Bay, Espiritu Santo and Torokina.

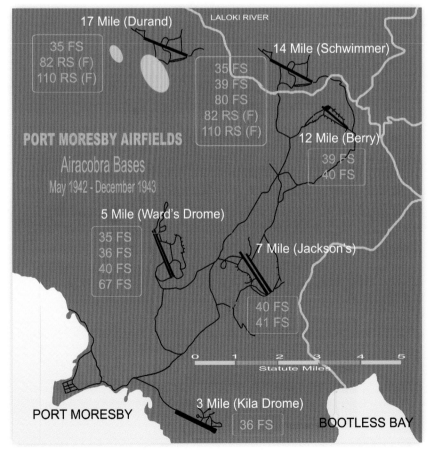

Port Moresby's six airfields hosted numerous Airacobra squadrons throughout the war, with squadrons sometimes moving locations depending on which tour they were on, space, availability and even the weather. The Seven-Mile and Three-Mile 'dromes were extant for the first Airacobra operations from April 1942 while the others were built throughout 1942.

Pacific Airacobra Squadrons
Main Deployments
USAAF Fifth & Thirteenth Air Forces

SQN	1942 M J J A S O N D	1943 J F M A M J J A S O N D	1944 J F M A M J
12		Guadalcanal, Munda, Torokina, Treasury Island	
35	Port Moresby, Milne Bay		
36	Port Moresby, Milne Bay, Tsile Tsile		
39	Port Moresby		
40	Port Moresby Tsile Tsile Nadzab Gusap		
41	Port Moresby Tsile Tsile Nadzab		
67	Guadalcanal Port Moresby Woodlark Torokina Green Island		
68	Guadalcanal Ondonga Segi Torokina		
70	Guadalcanal Ondonga Segi Torokina		
80	Port Moresby Milne Bay		
82	Port Moresby Nadzab Saidor Finschhafen Gusap		
110	Port Moresby Gusap Tadji		

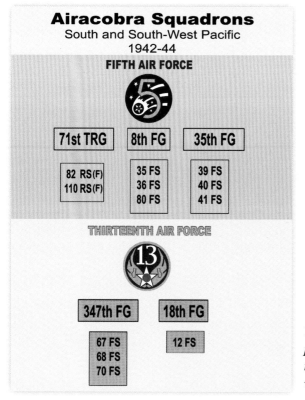

Airacobra Squadrons
South and South-West Pacific
1942-44

FIFTH AIR FORCE

71st TRG	8th FG	35th FG
82 RS(F) 110 RS(F)	35 FS 36 FS 80 FS	39 FS 40 FS 41 FS

THIRTEENTH AIR FORCE

347th FG	18th FG
67 FS 68 FS 70 FS	12 FS

The yellow bands indicate timelines for deployment and the main bases used by the Pacific Airacobra squadrons featuring in this volume. The timelines do not indicate short temporary deployments, such as rest periods in Australia or New Zealand or down-time for maintenance.

The command structure and parent Fighter Groups of all of the squadrons described in this volume.

Glossary

CN	Constructor's Number
CO	Commanding Officer
FS	Fighter Squadron
Hinomaru	The red disc on the Japanese flag representing the sun and also used as a roundel on Japanese aircraft.
IFF	Identification Friend or Foe
MIA	Missing in Action
PS	Pursuit Squadron
RAAF	Royal Australian Air Force
RNZAF	Royal New Zealand Air Force
RS(F)	Reconnaissance Squadron (Fighter)
TRG	Tactical Reconnaissance Group
US	United States
USAAC	United States Army Air Corps
USAAF	United States Army Air Force

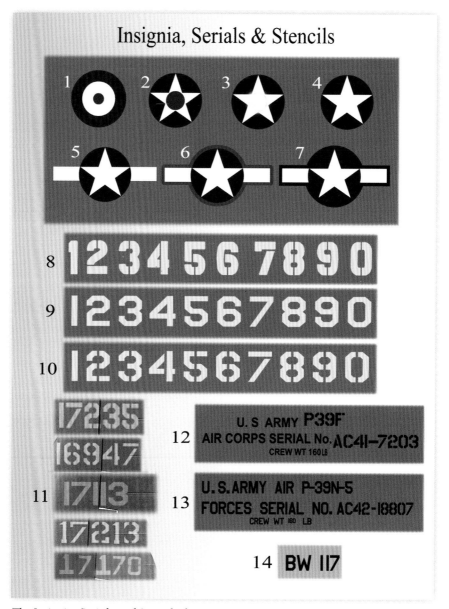

The Insignia, Serials and Stencils diagram as referenced in the text.

CHAPTER 1
Markings

National Insignia

A wide range of US insignia appeared on Pacific Airacobras, with colours faded and desaturated due to tropical wear. The ubiquitous US insignia of white star in blue circle with red centre in Example 2 (see the diagram titled Insignia, Serials and Stencils on page 12) has its pedigree in the pre-war era, the colours of which reflect those of the US flag. However, it became apparent during the heat of combat that the red circle, albeit small, could be confused with the Japanese *hinomaru*.

Accordingly, some individual pilots took the initiative of painting out the small circle. This often left a faint halo mark per Example 3. On 12 May 1942 the design with the red centre removed was formalised by technical orders issued from Washington. Nonetheless, some Pacific Airacobras were still exhibiting the red centre as late as December 1942, 67th FS P-400s in Guadalcanal and New Caledonia *inter alia* being routine offenders.

In April 1942, along with other manufacturers, Bell sought Washington's permission to omit the dark blue "US ARMY" lettering on the underneath of the wings. Although approved primarily as an economy measure to save paint, most extant airframes retained the marking throughout their service until retired from the field. Further specific comments on the US insignia in the examples shown in the *Insignia, Serials and Stencils* diagram are:

Example 1   British Roundel

This roundel appeared on most P-400s exported to the South Pacific being airframes redirected from the RAF. The first job after unpacking these P-400s was to apply the US insignia directly over the roundels, to the exact same size. However, note that roundels continued to appear when replacement wings were changed in the field without bothering to overspray the roundels.

Example 2   Pre-war to August 1942

This was the standard pre-war red circle-in-star applied to all USAAC aircraft leaving US factories until March 1942. Interim production lines caught between orders over sprayed the inner red roundels.

Example 3   Early 1942 onwards

This resulted from tropical wear of overspray of Example 2 roundels in the field. Several Airacobras retained the original Example 2 insignia on their wing undersides until retired from service.

Example 4   May 1942 onwards

This is the revised US insignia which appeared on all P-39D and P-39F models leaving Bell's factories May 1942 onwards.

Example 5   July 1943 onwards (no technical specification)

The standard star insignia in Example 4 was modified with a white bar by both the Fifth and Thirteenth Air Forces in the field.

Example 6   June through August 1943 (Specification AN-1-9A)

Several small batches of late N and Q model Airacobras were delivered to the theatre with red-bordered stars and bars which first appeared in June 1943, and often these borders were painted over immediately, or dark borders were applied to Example 5 insignia. New borders were applied with whatever paint stocks were at hand, varying from light blue to black.

Example 7   August 1943 (Specification AN-1-96)

Following complaints from the forward areas about the red surround "Star and Bar" new technical orders were issued to apply this final style, which became the standard USAAF insignia for the war's remainder. It appeared on P-39N-5 models and onwards including the P-39Q.

P-39 Serial Numbers

In August 1941 the US Army Air Corps issued Circular 100-4 instructing that all aircraft were to have their serial number applied in yellow to the fin. Although all USAAC serials began with the last two digits of the year of allocation, i.e. "41" for 1941, when applied the first digit was always omitted, along with the hyphen. Thus, for example, P-39D serial 41-6735 appears as 16735.

Bell Aircraft decided that the US Army would wish to apply their own serials, so early batches of P-39D-1s and P-39F-1s left the factory without them. The responsibility of applying the relevant serials fell to recipient units, a task often interpreted liberally, and which varied from unit to unit. Different calligraphy styles were applied, varying from hand-made stencils to more artistic painted applications. Five examples of differing styles are showcased as illustrated in Example 11, all extracted from photos. Some units such as the 70th FS in Fiji and the 12th FS in Guadalcanal were tardy in applying serials and continued to rely instead on the squadron number applied in the field.

There were technical orders pertaining to the shapes and sizes of serial numbers when painted as per Example 9, which appeared as stencilled as per Example 10. However, as demonstrated in the five field samples in Example 11, some units were more conformist than others. Constant repairs, new paint jobs and rudder replacements meant that new stencils were often applied in the field. Artistic license was sometimes seized by maintenance crews, creating unusual and deviant styles.

Bell commenced applying their own serials in the factory commencing with P-39D-1s in the 41-38XXX series. For reasons which are unclear, they adopted a unique stencil style per Example 8, being exactly nine inches high.

The British insignia is over-sprayed at Amberley in March 1942 on the top wing surface of a P-400. The consignment note attached to the crate is addressed to "Crew Chief P-400 AP332".

P-400 RAF Serials, Airframe and Batch Numbers

Around 260 P-400s originally destined for the RAF wound up in the inventories of the Fifth and Thirteenth Air Forces instead. Confusion exists between the British serial numbers which were applied under the tailplane per Example 14, their construction numbers, and their batch number. These numbers are interlinked in logical but disjointed sequences, e.g. British serial BW 114 was constructor's number CN14-306, but was allocated batch number 266.

The three-digit batch/consignment number was stencilled on wooden packing cases in black and on the P-400's tail in either black or white as per Profiles 38, 43 and 71. It is possible to deduce the British serial from the batch number, but only if the constructor's number is known as well. Markings have been further confused in past years when cursory research assumed that the last two or three digits of the British serial also served as squadron or "buzz" numbers. This did happen, but rarely (e.g. the 41st FS applied squadron numbers 170 through 175 for serials BW170 through BW175).

Another mistake made over the years, especially from wreck sites, is that the batch number on the tail represents the CN, confusing British serial identification. Likewise, CNs sometimes have been entered as tail numbers, further confusing the issue. Alternately, some genuine squadron numbers have been entered as serial numbers, British or otherwise, and vice versa. The scope for misidentification is more rife with the Airacobra than any other Allied airframe.

P-400s sent to the Pacific theatre fell in random batches between British serial ranges of AC103 to AC738, AP266 to AP383, BW100 to BW183 and BX135 to BX378. An eccentricity is that somehow two orphans - AH728 and AH736 – were also delivered to the theatre. These two airframes were unique as they were painted in RAF coastal command green/grey camouflage, an elusive quirk. The British serials of all P-400 profiles in this volume are confirmed either via photography or official records.

A freshly assembled P-400 British serial BW114 at RAAF Laverton. The white stencil 266 on the tail is a batch consignment number, whilst the airframe's construction number is 14-306.

USAAF Fuselage Serials

All P-39 models had a fuselage serial number identification stencilled forward and below the pilot's port cockpit door. The style changed slightly when the Army Air Corps became the Army Air Force: the change in airframe stencils is shown in Example 13 as compared to Example 12. In association, on 15 May 1942 all USAAC Pursuit Squadrons were redesignated as Fighter Squadrons.

Theatre Markings

Towards the end of 1943 Fifth Air Force fighters started appearing with white tailplanes and wing leading edges. These markings were applied so that Allied fighters could be readily identified from the air or ground. The practice did not spread widely into Thirteenth Air Force units although several white-tailed Fifth Air Force Airacobras were reassigned into Thirteenth Air Force units. The official directive was not promulgated until September 1943; however, some tails were painted as early as August 1943. Many were painted in water-based or acrylic paints which were particularly prone to weathering. Overall, the white theatre markings present an example of the Fifth Air Force leading by inventiveness, and Washington agreeing to the concept after it had been initiated.

Formation Markings

It was rare for Airacobra units to apply formation markings however the 67th FS did with its first batch of P-400s, painting the wing tips white.

Individual Markings and Art

Decorating aircraft with personalised markings was not sanctioned by Washington until August 1944, however, art and nicknames often appeared on Airacobras (or on most USAAF aircraft for that matter) as soon as they were unpacked from their crates. For these units isolated a long way from home it was a morale booster in harsh surroundings. Pilots came to feel that via such markings their airplane's individuality was secured and somehow made them safer. Such applications were tacitly supported by commanding officers. A sympathetic public back home well understood that such morale boosters would help win a war which presented as a clear-cut battle of good versus evil.

This P-400 encapsulates why so many Airacobra markings inaccuracies and misunderstandings have arisen over the years. It has an olive drab replacement rudder, elevators and ailerons; there is a black stencil 37 from when it served with the 39th FS (usually stencilled in white); a yellow forward fin tip and letter M from a tour with the 36th FS; and it has an 80th FS shark-mouth. When photographed over Port Moresby this P-400 was not assigned to a combat unit but to the Fifth Air Force replacement pool and is illustrated in Profile 73.

There was no shortage of inspiration to create nose art in the 1940s. The popular men's magazine *Esquire* was a source of choice, containing illustrations of lightly dressed females by artist Alberto Vargas. Another popular pick were comic characters from strips such as *Burma, Madame Shoo Shoo, Dragon Lady*, Milt Canniff's *Terry and the Pirates* and *Miss Lace* from the strip *Male Call*. Hollywood promoted the war effort in conjunction with the War Department, spawning a culture of victory illustrated with cartoons. Paints used for artistic pursuit were anything but standardised. Some were brought up from Australia, whilst others were "borrowed" from quartermasters, or traded with ground units for commodities. Mixing stocks of "Insignia Blue", yellow and red produced no end of colour variety.

The quality zinc chromate primer applied in Bell's factory influenced the longevity of paint schemes. The quality control of wartime factories focused on practical machines to win a war, and the olive drab paint scheme was applied hurriedly for reasons of practicality, not finesse. Coral and muddy airfields accelerated the weathering process. Tropical exposure changed the timbre of olive drab and desaturated the colour in the process, eventually resulting in dull matt grey brown.

Airacobra units themselves recorded scant details about their own markings or colour schemes simply because most lacked official approval. This detail is so deficient, that no unit records align "buzz" numbers or squadron letters against serial numbers, save the occasional maintenance log entry. Thus, the illustrations in this book rely almost exclusively on private records or photographs to align "buzz", tail, fuselage and cowl letters.

Squadron Insignia

In 1924 squadron insignia became subject to strict War Department authority. Pre-war designs submitted for approval were expected to be functional, depicting historical significance and importantly capable of being readily applied by personnel in the field. Policy statements of the time banned designs which implied death, destruction or gambling. Yet even by the early stages of the war, many Airacobra squadrons relished in insignia which exaggerated these very qualities. Squadron and/or group heraldry appeared in the form of emblems or motifs, and in the case of the Airacobra, mostly on the doors which were easily removed. It was common practice to swap doors following an accident.

With no shortage of creativity among the eager cadre of fighter pilots who took the Airacobra to war, it was inevitable that many of the pre-war staid squadron insignia were replaced or modified. Some squadrons were created at short notice with fresh insignia created shortly thereafter. In such cases the paint had long dried before Washington's formal imperator was issued. There were no formal rules for use of these insignia; the 39th Pursuit Squadron liberally applied their ("Aira") Cobra insignia to the doors of their fighters for the 1941 war games. However, once they reached New Guinea they were told they could not use the logo or the callsign "Cobra" for security reasons. A wide variety of other art quickly appeared on the 39th FS's doors, usually based around Walt Disney characters.

While security reasons were being cited on the front line, back in the USA the Oldsmobile Division of General Motors brandished the "Flying Buzzsaw" insignia of the 41st FS to promote war bonds and its production of Airacobra nose-cannon. Their posters even helpfully portrayed a squadron of P-400s decorated with the squadron insignia, again removed in the field on security grounds, with the callsign "Beaver" replacing "Buzzsaw". Nonetheless, these insignia were proudly painted on signs outside any headquarters tent or building in the field. On the other hand, the 12th FS painted their mailed fist logo on every aircraft on the first batch of P-39Ds they took to Christmas Island, then Guadalcanal. For reasons which remain unclear, the Thirteenth Air Force permitted more liberal insignia regimes than its Fifth Air Force counterparts.

The Emblems

The logos illustrated here were the ones used by these squadrons during the time they operated Airacobras. Many of these logos appeared in varying versions, were modified later on in the war and modified further still when some of these units fought in Korea and Vietnam. Some of these Airacobra units still exist today, the extant squadron still using similar insignia.

The relevant WWII squadron insignia are illustrated on page 20 and are described below:

- The logo of the 12th FS, featuring a fist clutching a lightning bolt. The name "Dirty Dozen" represents the squadron number twelve.

- The oval shape of the black and white panther emblem of the 35th FS.

- The "Flying Fiends" character of the 36th FS appeared in several guises, this one extracted from a badge made in Sydney, Australia.

- When the 39th Pursuit Squadron was chosen to be the first USAAC Squadron to operate the Airacobra, a Bell Aircraft Corporation artist designed this "Cobra in the Clouds" insignia, which was registered with the US Institute of Heraldry. Subsequently the squadron became officially termed "The Cobra Squadron". The insignia was liberally applied to all squadron Airacobra doors during the 1941 South Carolina manoeuvres in the US.

- When the 40th Pursuit Squadron was first activated on 22 December 1939 its first commander Captain Albert Clark designed a Red Devil insignia for an anticipated inventory of P-40Es. The insignia was redesigned into this circular format to fit on Airacobra doors when the type was operated by the squadron during the 1941 South Carolina manoeuvres in the US.

Numerous fade marks, oil spills and other wear markings exemplify the degree to which Airacobra airframes were affected by the harsh tropical weather and service conditions. This P-39K is having its guns serviced near Seven-Mile, Port Moresby.

Airacobra pilot Lieutenant Phil Shriver with the 40th FS logo at Port Moresby.

The sign for the 82ⁿᵈ Reconnaissance Squadron at Dobodura before they acquired their "Strafin' Saints" name.

A variant of the 35ᵗʰ FS Black Panther insignia outside the squadron's operations shack at 14-Mile, Port Moresby.

- The "Flying Buzzsaw" insignia of the 41st FS, also used by Oldsmobile to promote war bonds and its production of the Airacobra's nose-cannon.

- The 67th Pursuit Squadron "Fighting Cock" insignia was designed and donated to the squadron by Walt Disney. It was applied to many of the squadron's doors.

- The origins of the 68th Pursuit Squadron "Lightning Lancers" insignia are unclear. It was not officially approved until November 1944 however it was in use well before this date.

- The first 70th Pursuit Squadron insignia was a white knight chess piece superimposed over a chess board, however for unknown reasons it was not approved. The white knight theme was retained however in the approved version seen here.

Squadron insignia as discussed in the text, although a few of these were only used after Airacobras had been replaced by other types.

- The 80th FS was given the name "Headhunters" by squadron commander Major Edward Cragg in mid-1943. The original insignia design was drawn in pencil by crew chief Sergeant Yale Saffro. Note the aviator goggles on the face on this later version from which cloth patches were replicated in Sydney. The insignia was thus not in use during the squadron's Airacobra era.

- The 82nd Tactical Reconnaissance Squadron allocated itself the name "Strafin' Saints" in late 1944 although the origins of the art are unclear. Several sources erroneously apply the name to the squadron's parent group, the 71st Tactical Reconnaissance Group. Neither the name nor logo were in use during the Airacobra era.

- In late 1944 Major Rubel Archuleta, the new commander of the 110th Tactical Reconnaissance Squadron created the "Musketeers" logo. The logo was too late to appear on the squadron's P-39s, but later decorated the unit's P-40Ns and then later P-51s. The squadron had a goggled mule as its pre-war logo, however this was not approved and quietly discarded before the unit got to New Guinea.

The Oldsmobile advertisement which appeared in US magazines, showcasing the 41ˢᵗ FS emblem.

These airborne P-39Ks and Ds were taken flying westwards along Guadalcanal's northern coast not long after the 12th FS deployed there on 19 December 1942. Note that several still lack serial numbers.

12th Fighter Squadron

CHAPTER 2
12th Fighter Squadron "Dirty Dozen"

Constituted as the 12th Pursuit Squadron (Interceptor) on 20 November 1940, this squadron was serving with the Seventh Air Force when it was called forward from Christmas Island to Efate in the New Hebrides on 19 November 1942.

The squadron was part of the original plan to defend the sea lane supply route from the US to Brisbane via Hawaii. As such, it was intended that the squadron would defend Christmas Island some two thousand miles northeast of Fiji, the 68th FS would protect Tongatabu, the 70th FS would defend Fiji and the 67th FS would secure New Caledonia. The squadron redeployed to Fighter #2 on Guadalcanal on 19 December 1942 where it conducted operations until it moved to Kukum Field on Guadalcanal on 7 February 1943. At Guadalcanal it was reassigned to the 18th Fighter Group.

On 24 December 1942 the 12th FS made its first combat claim, two Zeros by squadron commander Major Paul Bechtel. The squadron was accompanying SBDs to bomb Munda when they unexpectedly met the Zeros overhead. These were a detachment of 21 No. 252 *Ku* Zeros which had arrived at Munda to take up station when it was opened to air operations on 23 December 1942. This detachment was accompanied by nine more Zeros from No. 204 *Ku*.

In the Solomons the squadron operated D, K and N model Airacobras and conducted escort missions, patrols and later ground attack and bombing missions. It subsequently operated from Treasury Island from 19 February until August 1944, after which it left the theatre when it moved to Mar 'drome in Dutch New Guinea.

During its time in the Pacific it served under various commanders; Major Paul Bechtel was replaced by Captain Theron Graves on 27 January 1943, then Captain Robert Kuehnle (26 February 1943), Bechtel again (7 March 1943), Captain Cyril Nichols (18 May 1943), Graves again (15 June 1943), Nichols again (11 July 1943), Graves again (1 August 1943), and Lieutenant Colonel Leland McGowan from 28 August 1943 until 11 Apr 1944. It then saw out its time in the theatre under the leadership of Captain Robert Smith. The squadron lost four pilots to combat during while operating Airacobras in the Pacific.

Markings

Ironically, the first squadron illustrated in this volume is the squadron whose markings are least photographed. At Christmas Island the batch of D models first issued had no serial painted on the fin, and some of these appeared in Guadalcanal still without serials. The squadron decorated the doors of all this first batch with the "Dirty Dozen" squadron logo of a fist clutching a red lightning bolt. Many applied female names in cursive script to the port gun cowl. As the Ds and Ks were gradually replaced by N models the squadron logo disappeared and was replaced by a three-digit numbering system.

12th Fighter Squadron

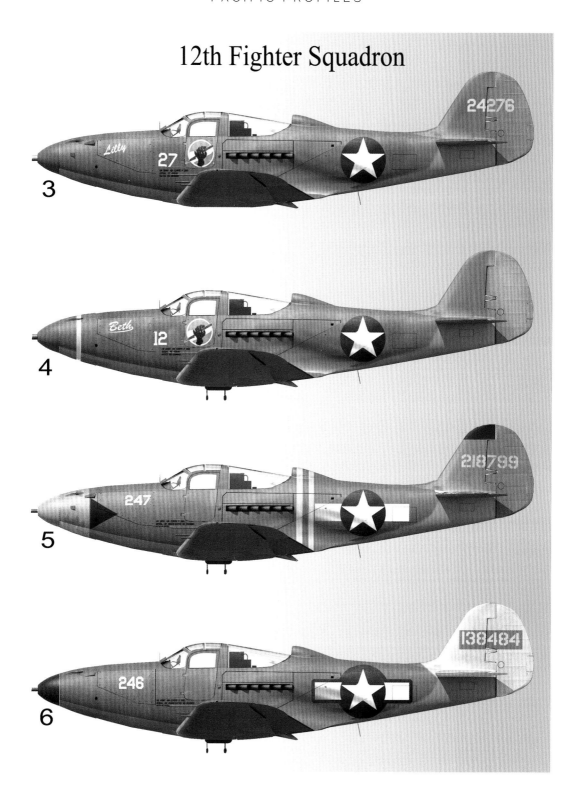

The squadron's early numbering system went from 1 through to 30, however this was changed in late 1943 when it was replaced by a three-digit system whereby the units operating from Torokina could be easily determined in the air; the first digit indicated the squadron to which the Airacobras were assigned: 200 series for the 12th FS, 300 series for the 70th FS and 400 series for the 68th FS.

The unit's most unusual Airacobra was one of the early model Ds which, when retired from combat, was stripped back to natural metal finish and was used as a hack on Guadalcanal with the name *Daisy Mae*, also painted with pin-up nose-art. This aircraft is illustrated in Profile 6 and see also the photo on page 118 when it was used as a hack.

(Profiles 1 and 2 are on page 22)

Profile 1: P-39K serial unknown, Christmas Island, November 1942

This Airacobra is profiled just before it transferred to Guadalcanal from Christmas Island where it was given an unknown squadron number. Note the unusual wave camouflage demarcation which was applied to some batches of K models.

Profile 2: P-39D serial unknown, *Innocent Imogene*, Christmas Island, November 1942

This Airacobra is profiled just before it transferred to Guadalcanal from Christmas Island where it was given an unknown squadron number.

Profile 3: P-39K-1 serial 42-4276, *Lilly*, 27, Fighter #2 (Guadalcanal), late December 1942

Profile 4: P-39D serial unknown, *Beth*, 12, Fighter #2 (Guadalcanal), late December 1942

This Airacobra was assigned to CO Paul Bechtel, indicated by the white band on the nose. The early leadership command stripe system within the squadron is not clearly understood.

Profile 5: P-39N-5 serial 42-18799, 247, Torokina, late 1943

The two stripes indicate this Airacobra was flown by then squadron commander, Lieutenant Colonel Leland McGowan. The extra white nose and black triangle and black tail tip were applied to make the aircraft more prominent in aerial formation. Sometime in early 1944 the tailplane was painted white as an IFF marking, with the serial masked off. It is likely this airframe was formerly operated by the Fifth Air Force.

Profile 6: P-39D-1 serial 41-38484, 246, Treasury Island, March 1944

A blue surround was added in the field to the national insignia and white bars were later added. Sometime in late 1943 the tail was painted white as an IFF marking, with the serial masked off.

The port side of Profile 10 at Milne Bay. A white circle with red surround on the door awaits unknown art.

In December 1942 P-400 BX174 is overhauled at 17-Mile, Port Moresby, after service with the 35th FS for reassignment to another unit.

CHAPTER 3
35th Fighter Squadron "Black Panthers"

Although three Airacobra squadrons from the 35th Pursuit Group arrived in Australia in late February 1942, exclusively equipped with P-400s, it was the 35th and 36th FS which first saw combat. On 26 April 1942 fifteen 35th PS P-39D and P-39Fs left Woodstock airstrip, north of Brisbane, Queensland, to become the first forward-deployed Airacobra squadron at Port Moresby to fight the Japanese. However, the flights ran afoul bad weather north of Cairns, became disorientated, and ran out of fuel. Two bellied in, three successfully landed along the Queensland coast, and two went missing around Cape Grenville, with all seven Airacobras lost.

On 30 April 1942 the first offensive Airacobra mission in New Guinea was led by Lieutenant Colonel Boyd "Buzz" Wagner. Conducted against the Japanese airfield at Lae, Wagner was actually assigned to Fifth Fighter Command but flew a 39th PS P-39D on the mission, as illustrated in Profile 90. A combined formation of seventeen 35th and 36th PS Airacobras launched from Port Moresby just after lunch. After hitting Lae the Airacobras headed for Salamaua where they strafed camouflaged supply caches. The squadron fought many Zeros during this period, and escorted C-47 transports delivering materiel to Australian soldiers at the mountainous outpost at Wau.

This first deployment of Port Moresby Airacobras was maintained by an advance detachment of about a hundred engineers from the 35th Service Squadron (the same squadron number is co-incidental). Complemented by the better-equipped 8th Service Group which arrived in the town on 30 July 1942, without hangars this group was nonetheless able to conduct major airframe maintenance at Port Moresby's airfields. Once repaired, airframes were reassigned to other units, complicating markings regimes no end.

On 26 June 1942, 39th and 40th FS Airacobras arrived at Port Moresby to relieve the 35th and 36th FS which returned to Australia for recuperation. The 40th FS based itself at Five-Mile, from which both the 35th and 36th FS had previously operated, but the 39th FS was split into two echelons between 12-Mile and 14-Mile. Following their leave period, on 21 September 1942 both the 35th and 36th FS deployed to Milne Bay to relieve RAAF Kittyhawks of Nos. 75 and 76 Squadrons. Their new stock was bolstered by a hodgepodge of replacement Airacobras delivered via Port Moresby.

After a break in Australia, the squadron returned to Port Moresby and Milne Bay in January 1943, followed by a return to Mareeba in north Queensland in late February until May 1943 where they continued using Airacobras for training until another return to Port Moresby.

The squadron's last combat loss was on 1 June 1942 when Lieutenant William Hosford was shot down near Port Moresby. The squadron's last operational Airacobra loss was when a P-39F ditched on 27 July 1943 near Port Moresby on a test flight. The squadron lost fifteen Airacobras to combat and a similar number to operational losses. During its time in New Guinea the 35th FS used the callsign "Brandy". The unit transitioned to P-40N Warhawks at Port Moresby's Kila 'drome in October 1943.

35th Fighter Squadron

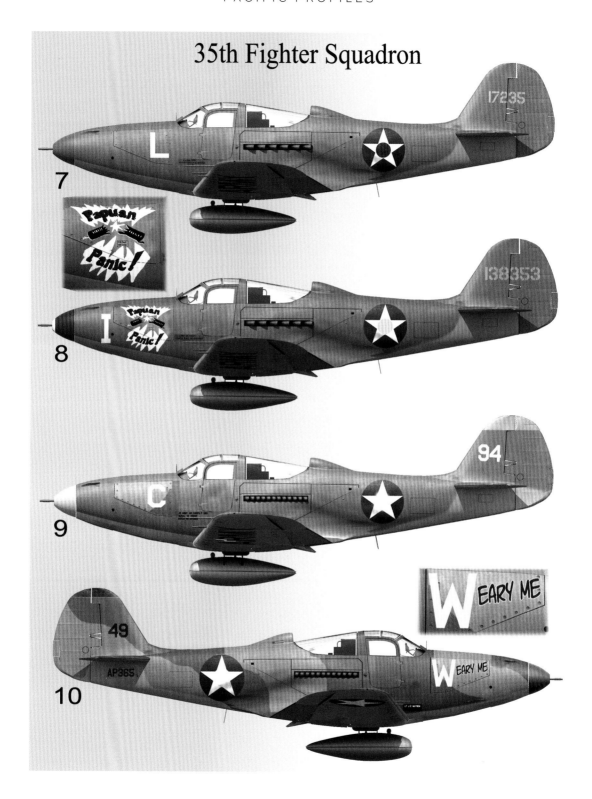

Markings

Each Airacobra was assigned an individual alphabetical letter, painted on the engine cowl panel in white or yellow depending on paint availability. The 35th FS retained a majority of P-39D and F airframes throughout its three Airacobra combat tours, however it also acquired a handful of P-400s from previous units. Some pilots painted their spinners, however there was no widespread use of one particular colour, and many retained the factory olive drab spinner, whilst others retained the colour of spinners from previous units.

Profile 7: P-39F-1 serial 41-7235, L, Port Moresby, April 1942

This was the highest serial-numbered P-39F delivered to Australia, unloaded at Brisbane wharves on 21 March 1942 from the SS *Merriweather Lewis*. It was assembled at Amberley and first delivered to the 80th Pursuit Squadron on 11 April 1942. It was then transferred as a replacement aircraft into the 35th FS in May 1942. A participant in the first New Guinea air battles, this airframe was later transferred to the RAAF on 15 July 1942 as A53-21. Subsequent to an operational accident, repairs were made to the propeller, flaps, and starboard wheel well fairing by RAAF No. 3 Air Depot at Amberley. It was then returned to USAAF control on 14 October 1943 after which it was used for liaison and training in Australia, then returned to the US on 5 March 1944 where it again served as a trainer. The fighter is illustrated as it appeared shortly after assigned into the squadron. The serial was applied with custom-made stencils a few days after being received.

Profile 8: P-39D-1 serial 41-38353, *Papuan Panic*, I, Milne Bay, September 1942

The markings of this fighter have been consistently misrepresented. Named by Lieutenant James Selzer, the nose art portrays a black exploding firecracker with the name in black-shadowed red letters. It was transferred to the 40th FS on 26 June 1942 when the 40th FS arrived at Port Moresby to relieve the 35th FS which then returned to Australia for leave. The 40th FS made no additional markings to the airframe apart from painting the spinner the squadron colour red with a narrow white tip. When the 40th FS returned to Australia for leave the 35th FS took it back on charge for their second combat tour. There was one white kill marking on the starboard side, just beneath the door, representing a No. 582 *Ku* Val claimed near Buna by Lieutenant Joseph McKeon on 7 December 1942. The fighter is portrayed as it appeared at Milne Bay in September 1942 during the squadron's second combat tour.

Profile 9: P-39D-1 unknown serial, 94, C, Woodstock, July 1942

The 35th FS was based at Woodstock, Queensland, for about a month commencing 29 June 1942 after completing its first New Guinea combat tour. It received this airframe in Australia from the 41st FS which had given it number 94 at Port Moresby and painted the fin tip white. Note that the forward gun cowling with letter C was a replacement panel from a P-400.

Profile 10: P-400 British serial AP 365, *Weary Me*, 49, W, Milne Bay, September 1942

This P-400 was assigned into the 35th FS when it returned to New Guinea after its stay at

35th Fighter Squadron

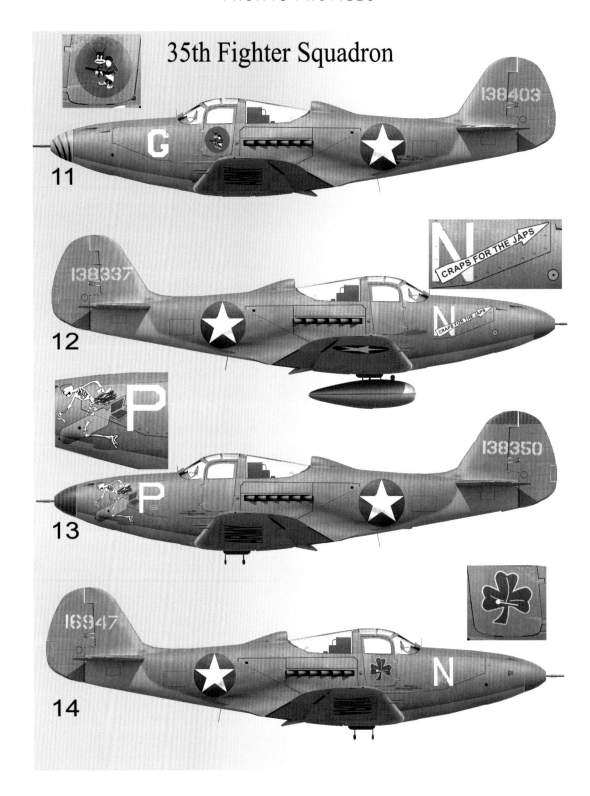

11 138403 · G

12 138337 · CRAPS FOR THE JAPS · N

13 138350 · P

14 16947 · N

Woodstock, Queensland. It received this airframe from the 41st FS (which allocated it squadron number 49) however the fighter had originally served with the 39th FS as per Profile 24. At Milne Bay the fighter was often flown by Lieutenant John Watson who was allocated the squadron letter "W" for his surname and named it *Weary Me*. The fighter is illustrated shortly after it was transferred into the 35th FS retaining its 39th FS markings of blue tail tip and spinner.

Profile 11
P-39D-1 serial 41-38403, G, Milne Bay, September 1942

This Airacobra was assigned to Captain Todd "Tom" Dabney and was the only one in the squadron decorated with a spiral spinner. The critter in the blue circle which decorated the port door was inspired by similar nose art carried on 22nd BG B-26 *Calamity Charlie* which Dabney had seen in Port Moresby. On the morning of 18 May 1942, Dabney claimed a G4M1 near Port Moresby whilst flying this fighter.

Profile 12
P-39D-1 serial 41-38337, *Craps for the Japs*, N, Milne Bay, September 1942

The name *Craps for the Japs* is a play on the card game Craps, and was a name also used by several other aircraft in the Fifth Air Force inventory including a B-17. The fighter was reassigned to another squadron in late 1942 and replaced by another Airacobra allocated the letter N per Profile 14.

Profile 13
P-39D-1 serial 41-38350, P, Milne Bay, September 1942

Often flown by Lieutenant Robert Parker, the letter P represented his surname. The fighter carried this creative nose-art but remained unnamed throughout its combat career. It had a red spinner and tail tip from a previous tour with the 40th FS.

Profile 14
P-39D-15 serial 41-6947, N, Port Moresby, May 1943

Accepted into the USAAF on 22 October 1941, this Airacobra was crated and shipped to Australia aboard the SS *Mormacsea*, arriving in Brisbane on 8 March 1942 as part of Project X, one of 53 Airacobras originally destined to reinforce the Philippines. It was transported by truck to Amberley RAAF base where it was assembled by No. 3 Air Depot, RAAF. It had its serial applied with hand-cut stencils a few days after assembly. After serving at least one combat tour with the 35th FS it was earmarked for the RAAF but never delivered, before being returned to USAAF inventory on 4 October 1943. It was subsequently scrapped at Amberley in 1944. Although a three-leaf clover decorated the starboard door, the fighter was never named.

The 35*th* FS flight-line at Milne Bay. Captain Tom Dabney's "G" per Profile 11 is at far right.

An engineer is undoing Tzus fasteners in preparation to remove the gun panel on Profile 12 at Milne Bay.

P-400 Weary Me, the Subject of Profile 10 at Milne Bay.

The subject of Profile 8 at Port Moresby.

Lieutenant Robert Parker at Milne Bay with Subject of Profile 13.

Lieutenant Irving Erickson with Profile 17 at Port Moresby.

CHAPTER 4
36ᵗʰ Fighter Squadron "Flying Fiends"

The 36ᵗʰ FS holds several distinctions in terms of Airacobra operations; it conducted the first Airacobra combat of the Pacific war which occurred on 6 April 1942 near Port Moresby, it operated the type in New Guinea longer than any other unit (from April 1942 until November 1943, converting to N and Q models in mid-1943) and it also operated the P-400 longer than any other unit in New Guinea, losing four in operations as late as August 1943.

After arriving at Brisbane on 6 March 1942, the 36ᵗʰ FS was transported to nearby Camp Ascot where they stayed for a week. They were then transported 33 miles inland to the RAAF training school at Lowood airfield on 13 March 1942. The squadron's Airacobras flew to Antil Plains southeast of Townsville on Easter Saturday 4 April 1942, where there were two airfields which they shared with 33ʳᵈ BS B-26 Marauders. The following day six Airacobras accompanied these bombers to Port Moresby where they joined No. 75 Squadron, RAAF, Kittyhawks to experience combat operations. The detachment was drawn from the squadron's most experienced pilots: Lieutenants William Meng (acting squadron commander), Charles Faletta (D Flight Leader), Paul Brown (A Flight Leader), Robert Harriger (B Flight Leader), Carl Taylor (C Flight Leader) and James "Hoot" Bevlock.

Upon arrival in Port Moresby's circuit area Faletta was first to land on 5 April 1942, making P-39 serial 41-6951 the first Airacobra to land in New Guinea during WWII (see Profile 89). Meng and Faletta engaged G4M1 Betty bombers and Zeros during a mid-morning raid on 6 April, during which both pilots' 37mm cannon failed to fire. The 36ᵗʰ FS detachment returned to Antil Plains five days later.

Following the first delivery flight fiasco of 26 April 1942 (see Chapter 3), on 1 May 1942 a second delivery flight by six 36ᵗʰ FS Airacobras underwent a similar fate. They left Townsville and headed for Port Moresby via Horn Island, but similar bad weather disorientated the flight just like the week prior. As a result, two Airacobras bellied in, three force-landed on Cape York Peninsula, and one pilot was killed when his fighter cartwheeled on landing.

On 1 May 1942 Lieutenant Donald McGee flying P-39D *Miss Nemesis*, scored the 36ᵗʰ FS' first confirmed victory when he shot down a Model 21 Tainan *Ku* Zero flown by FPO2c Arita Yoshisuke. After several weeks of intense combat on 26 June 1942 the 39ᵗʰ and 40ᵗʰ FS relieved the 35ᵗʰ and 36ᵗʰ FS at Port Moresby. The 35ᵗʰ and 36ᵗʰ FS then returned to Australia for a rest period, moving to Garbutt Field, Townsville, on 30 June.

On 14 September 1942 the 36ᵗʰ FS moved to Milne Bay where it once again fought alongside the 35ᵗʰ FS. Upon completion of this combat tour on 22 February 1943 the squadron transferred to Mareeba for recuperation. Shortly after returning to New Guinea, in June 1943 the unit received a batch of new P-39Q-5 and then P-39Q-10 Airacobras which it operated until November 1943. These came with 20mm cannon gun packs for the wings for low-level attack, but these were not used by the squadron. Instead, its missions were mainly transport escorts and patrols, as aerial combat was left to the more modern P-38Fs operated by the 39th FS. In November 1943 the squadron commenced transition to P-47Ds which they flew briefly before converting to P-38s in early 1944.

Markings

Similar to its sister squadron the 35th FS, each Airacobra was assigned an individual alphabetical letter, painted on the engine cowl panel usually in white, or sometimes yellow depending on paint availability. However, many Airacobras in the combat theatre did not receive a letter until towards the end of May 1942 as illustrated in Profile 15. Many Airacobras had their tail tips and spinners later painted yellow as a squadron identifier to the extent that the 36th FS was sometimes referred to as the "Yellow-Nose Squadron" around Port Moresby. The squadron retained a majority of P-39D and F airframes throughout its early combat tours, however it also acquired around five P-400s which they operated until August 1943 for escort duties.

A new markings regime was instituted when the 36th FS took delivery of its P-39Qs in June 1943. The serial numbers were masked off and the entire tailplane painted white in accordance with the Fifth Air Force IFF requirements. The single star insignia had two white bars added, and a white band was applied around the nose. All spinners were painted white, and the usual alphabetical letter was applied on the gun access panel, but in smaller size and thicker calligraphy than for the previous suite of D and F models.

The name Miss Helen the Flying Jenny as applied by Lieutenant George Welch per Profile 17.

Lieutenant Leonard Marks with Profile 16 at Milne Bay.

An unknown pilot poses on the wing of Profile 15.

36th Fighter Squadron

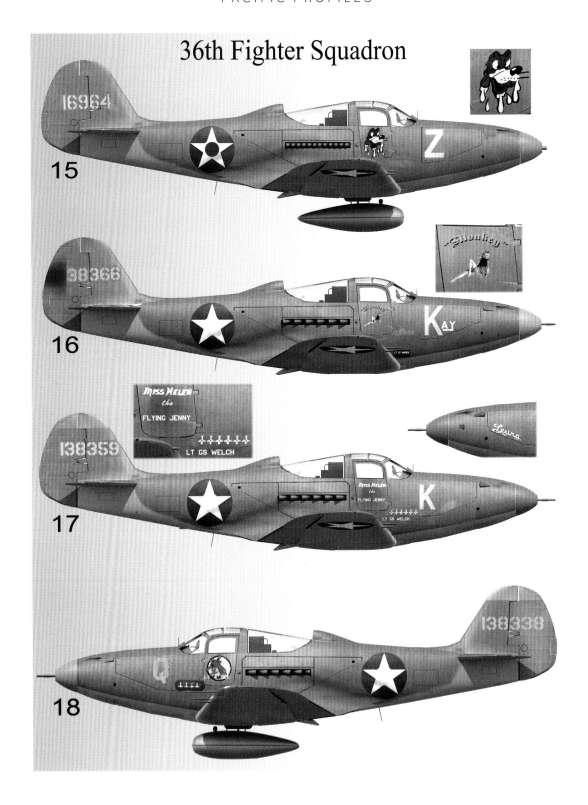

Profile 15: P-39D-15 serial 41-6964, Z, Port Moresby, May 1942

This Airacobra was in the first batch to arrive at Port Moresby and soon had its starboard door decorated with a fierce slobbering dog. The letter Z was applied around the end of May 1942, and the airframe was eventually scrapped at Amberley in 1944.

Profile 16: P-39D-1 serial 41-38366, *Kay*, K, Milne Bay, September 1942

This Airacobra was named by Lieutenant Leonard Marks who added two letters to the squadron letter K for the name of his girlfriend, Kay. The starboard door was painted with a Vargas calendar girl nicknamed *Monkey*, although it is unknown whose initiative this was. The fighter was transferred to an unknown squadron sometime in mid-1942 and is profiled following a rudder repair where the first letter of the serial was painted over.

Profile 17: P-39D-1 serial 41-38359, *Leura / Miss Helen the Flying Jenny*, K, Port Moresby and Milne Bay, September-December 1942

This Airacobra was first assigned to Lieutenant Irving Erickson who named it *Leura*. It was photographed at Kila 'drome with crew chief Sergeant EA Matteo when first assigned. Lieutenant George Welch took it over and flew it often during the Milne Bay tour, naming it *Miss Helen the Flying Jenny*. On 7 December 1942, exactly one year after Pearl Harbor during which Welch had fought Japanese carrier pilots, he claimed two No. 582 *Ku* D3A1 Vals and a Zero when flying this P-39. These claims northeast of Buna made Welch an ace.

Profile 18: P-39D-1 serial 41-38338, *Nip's Nemesis II*, Q, Port Moresby and Milne Bay, June-September 1942

This Airacobra replaced the first *Nip's Nemesis*, P-39D 41-6941, which was written off following combat on 1 May 1942. Named by Lieutenant Donald McGee this second airframe survived three combat tours and was eventually scrapped. *Nip's Nemesis II* carried a circular depiction of a demon's hand clutching crushed Zeros. McGee personalised the depiction by having his name interwoven into the artwork.

Subsequent to the war, McGee remained firmly at odds with official records in relation to how many Japanese he shot down when flying Airacobras. Regardless, McGee's performance at this early juncture in the theatre was impressive, and his confirmed kill of 1 May 1942 over Port Moresby marked the demise of Tainan *Kokutai* pilot FPO2c Arita Yoshisuke.

After McGee finished his combat tour, *Nip's Nemesis II* was transferred to the 41st FS where it was allocated squadron number 71. This P-39 was later scrapped in New Guinea or Australia. The fighter was still flying in 1943 as Lieutenant Dugan Woodring claimed a Zero when flying it on 12 April 1943 over Port Moresby. The four kill markings which overpaint the serial block represent McGee's four 1942 claims from 1 May, 29 May (two claims) and 15 September.

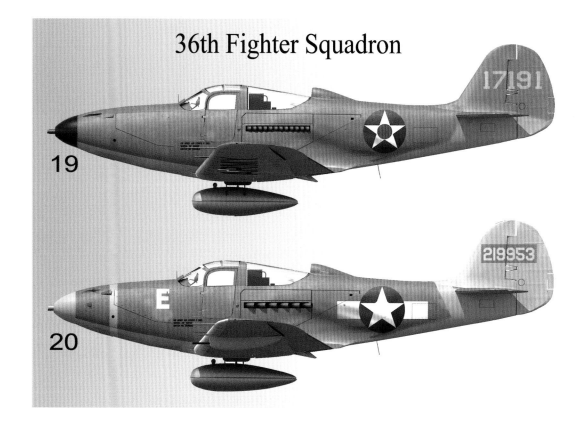

36th Fighter Squadron

Profile 19: P-39D-1 serial 41-7191, Port Moresby, early May 1942

At around 0915 on 18 May 1942 this Airacobra was one of several which attacked a formation of No. 4 *Ku* Betty bombers. Lieutenant Charles Chapman was flying it on the mission and remains MIA. The wreckage was discovered in 2001 in foothills north of Port Moresby and the site indicates clearly that it flat spun into the ground where the wreckage remains largely integrous. Neither cockpit door was present at the site indicating the likelihood Chapman either bailed out or was flung out due to centripetal force. Examination of the wreckage provides detailed evidence of the illustrated large unique serial font painted on the airframe. The propeller spinner was painted semi-gloss black. No squadron letter had yet been applied when the fighter was lost.

Profile 20: P-39Q-5 serial 42-19953, E, Port Moresby, June 1943

This Airacobra was among the first batch of Q models supplied to the 36th FS in June 1943. The markings were universally applied, i.e. the conformity of calligraphy indicates the entire fleet was likely marked by one person as opposed to the earlier D and F Airacobras each of which was individually decorated. The fighter is profiled with a gun pack which were first attached upon delivery, however, they were later removed and reattached when they were distributed between the 82nd and 110th RS(F).

Freshly painted P-39Ns at Port Moresby just after their delivery in late June 1943. Profile 20 appears on the far left, while squadron letters S, I and R are also visible.

Airacobra "D" with yellow spinner and tail tip. It previously served with the 39th FS as "32", which is still visible on the fin.

Lieutenant Charles King and Profile 23 at Woodstock, Queensland.

CHAPTER 5
39th Fighter Squadron "Cobras"

The 39th, 40th and 41st Pursuit Squadrons disembarked at Brisbane on 25 February 1942 from the liner SS *Ancon*. The 39th PS was commanded by Major Jack Berry, and sailed for Melbourne on 4 March 1942, docking four days later. The squadron's P-400s were meanwhile assembled at Amberley. From Melbourne the squadron travelled by train to Ballarat, where the personnel were billeted in civilian homes. The rail journey then continued to Mount Gambier in South Australia where the squadron arrived on 17 March.

At Mount Gambier the 39th FS received new P-400s and trained on them for a few weeks before moving to Woodstock airfield in Queensland on 20 April. The squadron was based at Woodstock for nearly two months, where it prepared for a deployment to New Guinea. During this period the squadron was redesignated from a Pursuit to a Fighter Squadron on 15 May.

After training at Woodstock, the 39th FS's Airacobras flew to Port Moresby on 2 June where they were dispersed between the 14-Mile and 12-Mile 'dromes. During this first tour the squadron fought numerous combat engagements defending Port Moresby from Japanese bomber and fighter attacks from Lae and Rabaul.

On the morning of 4 August 1942, the squadron CO Jack Berry was killed during a training exercise. His P-39D was toting a 250-pound practice bomb, trying to hit the shipwreck SS *Pruth* aground on an outer reef off Port Moresby. Bombing with a P-39 was then a new concept, and Berry's Airacobra suffered structural failure when the bomb skipped back and hit his fighter, driving it into the sea. Major Francis Royal took his place as 39th FS CO, and 12-Mile 'drome was later renamed Berry Field in his honour.

On 15 August 1942 the squadron's Airacobras were distributed among Port Moresby's other P-39 squadrons, mainly the 80th FS. The pilots then headed to Antil Plains in Queensland to take up training on P-38 Lightings, becoming the first Fifth Air Force squadron to operate that type. During its brief combat tour of around ten weeks the 39th FS lost ten Airacobras to combat and seven to operations and training accidents, four of which were in Australia.

In New Guinea the 39th FS used the callsign "Outcast", even though upon arrival they strongly preferred to use "Cobra" to reflect their squadron insignia. However, use of "Cobra" was banned on security grounds shortly after they arrived. Furthermore, they were also ordered to remove the circular cobra squadron insignia which decorated the doors of their mounts. With comprehensible indignation, many pilots treated all callsigns with impertinence for several weeks following the ban.

Markings

The 39th FS initially predominantly operated P-400s although it also had nine P-39Ds and Fs assigned to it during its last few weeks of operating the type. Squadron numbers ranged from

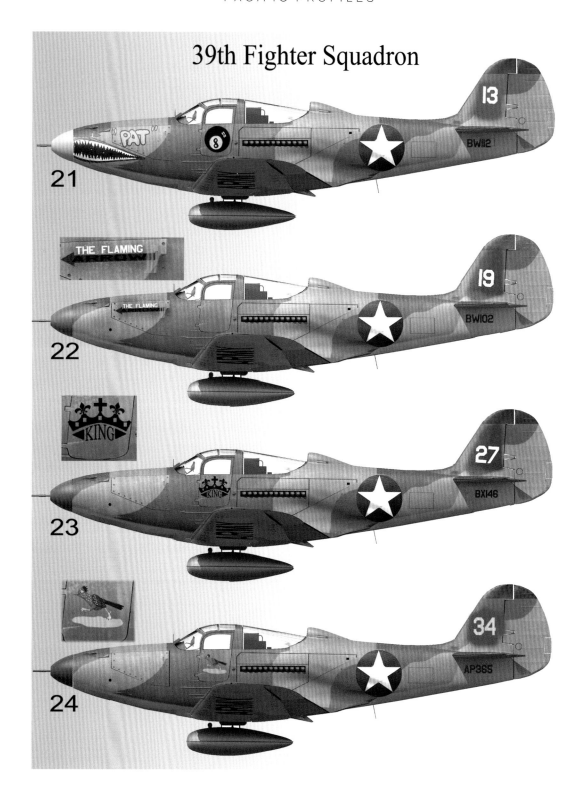

39th Fighter Squadron

10 to 39, a numerical sequence later carried through to their P-38s and stencilled in large white numerals on the fin. The tips of the vertical stabiliser and spinners, with some exceptions, were painted royal blue, the squadron colour.

Profile 21: P-400 British serial BW112, *Pat / Wahl Eye II*, 13, 12-Mile 'drome, August 1942

This Airacobra was named by Lieutenant Eugene Wahl after he force-landed the original *Wahl Eye* on 9 June 1942 southeast of Port Moresby near the village of Rigo. On 26 August 1942 Lieutenant Gerald Rogers was shot down in this replacement *Wahl Eye II* which also carried nose art and the name *Pat* on the port side as illustrated. Shot down by a Model 32 Zero near Pongani on New Guinea's northern coast, Rogers was strafed when he ditched, but was later assisted by friendly natives and missionaries to get back to Port Moresby via Wanigela. The *Wahl Eye II* starboard side artwork can be seen in the photo on page 46.

Profile 22: P-400 British serial BW102, *The Flaming Arrow*, 19, 14-Mile 'drome, June 1942

Lieutenant Curran "Jack" Jones named this Airacobra *The Flaming Arrow*, and it was allocated squadron number 19. The aircraft is profiled just after the nose art paint had dried at 14-Mile 'drome. When the 39th FS moved to Antil Plains, near Townsville, BW102 was transferred to the 80th FS where it was decorated with shark's teeth markings, and allocated the squadron letter K. This P-400 wound up in the Port Moresby boneyard by 1943 where it was scrapped post-war.

Profile 23: P-400 British serial BX146, *King*, 27, 14-Mile 'drome, July 1942

Lieutenant Charles King took delivery of this P-400 at Mount Gambier and flew it up to Woodstock near Townsville from Melbourne, refueling at Albury, New South Wales, *en route*. The distinctive door art characterised his surname, and the fighter was transferred to the 36th FS when the squadron's Airacobra inventory was redistributed to other squadrons when it returned to Antil Plains at the end of July 1942 in preparation to transition to P-38s. The 36th FS gave it the letter "D" however sometime after this it was transferred to the 80th FS which was operating it as late as February 1943.

Profile 24: P-400 British serial AP365, 34, 14-Mile 'drome, July 1942

An unknown pilot had this road-runner bird painted on the port door. When the 39th FS returned to Australia in July 1942 this P-400 was transferred to the 41st FS which allocated it squadron number 49. Then, by September it was operating with the 35th FS named as *Weary Me* per Profile 10.

The starboard side of Profile 21 stuck in Port Moresby mud.

BX154, squadron number 28, seen at Horn Island when later serving with the 36th FS.

39th FS P-400 squadron number 21 (unknown British serial) with its pilot at 14-Mile, Port Moresby.

39th FS P-400 squadron number 41 (unknown British serial) at 12-Mile, Port Moresby.

40ᵗʰ FS P-39D "7" was often flown by Lieutenant Eugene Deboer, seen with the Airacobra at 12-Mile around December 1942.

CHAPTER 6
40th Fighter Squadron "Fightin' Red Devils"

The 39th, 40th and 41st Pursuit Squadrons disembarked at Brisbane on 25 February 1942 from the liner SS *Ancon*, as described in the previous chapter. While at Mount Gambier the 40th FS received an influx of eight P-40E pilots who had served in Java with the 17th PS (Provisional). On the evening of 31 March the squadron boarded a train destined for Camden, New South Wales, in order to provide air cover near Sydney in case of an attack by Japanese aircraft carriers which did not materialise. The ground echelon departed Camden on 14 April and reached Townsville three days later. They were then transported to Antil Plains that same afternoon via truck where they encamped with the 36th FS, which departed for Port Moresby a few days later.

Towards the end of April 1942, the 40th FS incorporated a substantial contingent of enlisted men; however, few were qualified for airframe maintenance. On 2 June 1942 both the 39th and 40th FS moved to Port Moresby area to relieve the 35th and 36th FS. At Port Moresby the 40th FS's Airacobras were primarily based at 12-Mile with a brief deployment to Seven-Mile 'drome. After a period of intense combat, the squadron's pilots returned to Townsville on 29 August for recuperation and to re-equip, returning to Port Moresby on 5 December 1942. Following another break in Australia the 40th FS took up station at both at Moresby then Tsili Tsili from 25 August to 15 October 1943 before moving on to Nadzab and Gusap. At Nadzab on 23 November 1943 the squadron's Airacobras performed an airshow for a United Service Organization troupe led by Hollywood star Gary Cooper.

By February 1943 the 40th FS was operating ten P-39Ks and 14 P-39Ds with one P-400 assigned for training purposes. It took delivery of 23 P-39N Airacobras in August 1943 and later a handful of Q models, transferring all its D and K models to service units and the Fifth Air Force replacement pool.

During its time in New Guinea the 40th FS used the callsigns "Lepar" or "Dewlap". The squadron operated Airacobras until early December 1943 before transitioning to P-47Ds. The squadron lost 30 Airacobras in Australia and New Guinea: 13 to combat and the rest to operational or training losses. Captain Hubert Egenes was commanding officer from 16 May until 5 October 1942, Captain Harvey Scandrett from 8 October to 21 November 1942; Captain Malcolm Moore from 22 Nov 1942 to 25 April 1943; and Captain Thomas Winburn from 26 April to 10 November 1943.

Markings

A ubiquitous feature of squadron markings was a red tail tip and red spinner, reflecting the squadron colour. Airacobras were identified by a number in the 1 to 50 range, usually painted on the gun cowl and sometimes the fin too.

40th Fighter Squadron

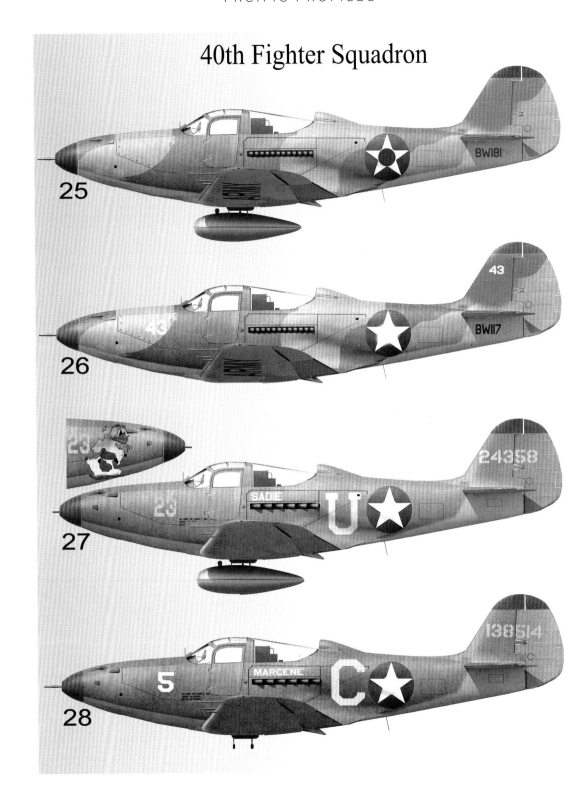

Around early to mid-1943 some flights in the 40th and 41st FS applied large alphabetical letters in either yellow or white to the rear of the exhaust manifolds. These did not replace squadron numbers but were used to assist aerial identification. These were unrelated to the alphabetical system employed by the 35th and 36th FS which applied the letters, slightly smaller, on the gun cowl. Examples can be seen in Profiles 27 & 28.

Profile 25: P-400 British serial BW181, unknown squadron number, Seven-Mile 'drome, July 1942

Lieutenant Garth Cottam went missing in this P-400 in bad weather over the Buna area on 22 July 1942. Most references record him as lost the following day however Townsville was not notified until 23 July of his loss, in a signal which records his loss as occurring around 0700 on the morning of 22 July 1942.

Profile 26: P-400 British serial BW117, 43, Seven-Mile 'drome, July 1942

On 11 July 1942 Lieutenant Edward Gignac departed Seven-Mile 'drome near Port Moresby during a scramble to intercept Japanese bombers. When he reached 15,000 feet, he experienced engine failure and crashed-landed near 30-Mile 'drome injuring himself. Gignac was later returned to the United States.

Profile 27: P-39K-1 serial 42-4358, *Sadie*, 23, U, 12-Mile, Port Moresby, February 1943

The first K model P-39s to serve with the Fifth Air Force arrived in December 1942. Assigned to First Lieutenant William McDonough, the fightin' *Donald Duck* motif appeared only on the starboard nose. McDonough claimed two Ki-43-I fighters with this fighter on 6 February 1943 over Wau, and it is portrayed as it appeared then. Two of the four Japanese losses included 11th *Sentai* commanding officer Major Suguira Katsuji and *chutaicho* Captain Miyabashi Shigenori. McDonough was later killed near Port Moresby on 22 April 1944 during an unsuccessful P-47D bail-out.

Profile 28: P-39D-2 serial 41-38514, *Marcene*, 5, C, 12-Mile, Port Moresby, February 1943

In early 1943 several of the squadron's pilots started naming their aircraft after girlfriends or wives. *Marcene* was not lost to operations or combat.

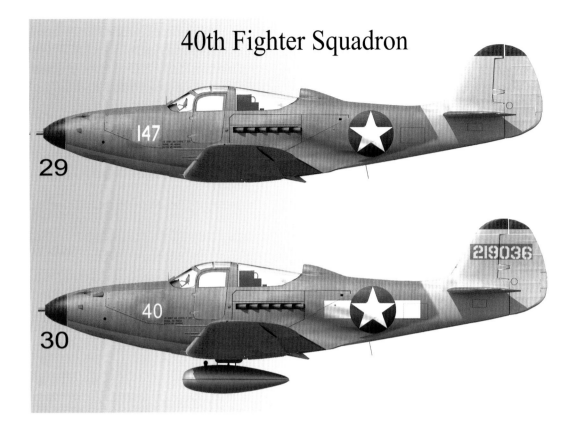

40th Fighter Squadron

29

30

Profile 29: P-39F-1 serial 41-7147, 147, Tsili Tsili, August 1943

Unusually, after painting over the serial number with the white tail marking, on this particular P-39 the last three digits of the serial were used as the squadron number. Note that the star insignia remained without white bars when it first arrived at Tsili Tsili.

Profile 30: P-39N-5 serial 42-19036, 40, Berry 'drome, August 1943

This P-39 was destroyed at Berry 'drome following a landing accident there when piloted by squadron commander Major Thomas Winburn.

Profile 27 at 12-Mile 'drome, Port Moresby.

Lieutenant Phil Shriver poses with his early P-39D-1 Anon III "10" at 12-Mile. The unusual nose-art (not fully visible) was a split character, the top half being a monkey carrying a pistol.

40th FS "27" was P-39D-1 serial 41-38349, seen here at Seven-Mile.

The port side of Profile #27 at 12-Mile while having its hydraulic fluids drained and changed.

40ᵗʰ FS P-39Ks "15" and "11" fly down the Markham Valley near Nadzab in November 1943.

Brand new K model Airacobra 42-4351 of the 40th FS is test-flown from 12-Mile, Port Moresby, in December 1942 shortly after being allocated squadron number 15.

Profile 33 as decorated by Lieutenant David Latane. Latane baled out of this P-400 in February 1943. The fighter replaced Profile 9, which was transferred to the 39th FS.

This P-39N "X" replaced Profile 33. The fighter is being slung via its hoist points in Port Moresby by the 27th Air Depot.

CHAPTER 7
41ˢᵗ Fighter Squadron "Flying Buzzsaws"

The 41ˢᵗ FS was first constituted as the 41ˢᵗ PS on 22 December 1939 and activated on 1 February 1940. It arrived in Australia with the 39ᵗʰ and 40ᵗʰ Pursuit Squadrons at Brisbane on 25 February 1942 on the liner SS *Ancon*. The squadron moved to Archerfield airfield south of Brisbane where it stayed until 8 March, before moving to Mount Gambier where it received recently assembled P-400s.

On 6 April the 41ˢᵗ PS traveled by train to Bankstown airport, west of Sydney, and the unit was redesignated the 41ˢᵗ Fighter Squadron on 15 May. On 29 May a Japanese floatplane carried out a night reconnaissance flight over Sydney which one of the unit's Airacobras tried unsuccessfully to intercept. On Sunday 8 June the Japanese submarine *I-24* surfaced off Sydney and opened fire with its deck gun on the city. At Bankstown Lieutenant George Cantello scrambled in P-400 BW140 to hunt the submarine. However, after climbing to 1,000 feet his engine failed just after take-off and he crashed about three miles southwest of the field. Cantello died in the crash.

The 41ˢᵗ FS moved to Seven-Mile, Port Moresby, on 20 July 1942 where it exclusively operating P-400s until December 1942. Some of the squadron's first missions were strafing Japanese troop positions along with Kokoda Track. It received a small batch of P-39Ks in December 1942 and later P-39Ds from the 8ᵗʰ FG inventory. The squadron returned to Australia in early 1943 for recuperation. By February 1943 it was back in Port Moresby, where it was operated five P-400s, nineteen P-39Ds and one P-39K. Its inventory changed again only two months later when it was operating a dozen P-400s and ten P-39Ds.

In July 1943 the 41ˢᵗ FS traded its entire inventory for 25 P-39Ds, then moved operations to Tsili Tsili the following month, then Nadzab in December 1943. Its last airframe loss was due to an accident on 13 January 1944 when an N model suffered a nose wheel collapse at Saidor a few days after the strip was opened. The squadron commenced transition to P-47Ds at Nadzab at the end of that same month, with all of its P-39N and Q models reassigned between the 82ⁿᵈ and 110ᵗʰ RS(F). During its fifteen months in New Guinea it used the callsign "Beaver", or sometimes "Flatter". The squadron lost eleven Airacobras to combat and fourteen to operations including weather related losses.

Markings

The 41ˢᵗ FS allocated squadron numbers by maintenance flights, with the following numbers confirmed as appearing on the squadron's Airacobras: 70, 71, 71, 72, 73, 74, 75, 76, 80, 81, 83, 84, 85, 90, 91, 92, 93, 94, 95, 170, 171, 172, 172, 174, 175, 182 and 359. The last three digits of the P-400 British serials for BW170 to BW175 were used for numbers 170 through 175, serving the purpose of differentiating P-39s from P-400s. When an aircraft was lost its number was re-used. Several other P-400s used the last two digits of the British serial as the squadron number, 94 from AP 294 and 83 from BW 183 being examples.

41st Fighter Squadron

The squadron was divided into Red, White, Blue and Yellow flights; however, fighters were mixed among these flights and pilot rosters were random. Thus, pilots often shared their "assigned" fighter. On some days when operational activity was particularly busy an additional Green flight was added.

P-400s were delivered to the theatre with white spinners and these were often left white. The squadron colour of yellow was often applied to spinners and the tips of fins, although earlier deliveries of P-400s often had their fins painted white instead of yellow.

Around early to mid-1943 some flights in the 40th and 41st FS applied large alphabetical letters in either yellow or white to the rear of the exhaust manifolds. This was to assist aerial identification, and the letters did not replace the squadron numbers. These were unrelated to the alphabetical system used by the 35th and 36th FS which applied the letters, slightly smaller, on the gun cowl. Examples can be seen in Profiles 33, 39, 41 and 42.

Profile 31: P-400 British serial BW172, *Tojo*, 172, Seven-Mile, November 1942

This P-400 was assigned to Lieutenant Fred Harries whose nickname was "Tojo". He was named thus because his comrades thought that his short black hair and moustache made him appear Japanese. From northern Wisconsin, both Harries and his mount survived the war without mishap. The squadron number replicated the last three digits of the British serial.

Profile 32: P-400 British serial BW183, 83, Seven-Mile, December 1942

This Airacobra was one of two 36th FS P-400s which attempted to intercept an Emily flying boat during the Townsville air raid on the evening of 28 July 1942. It was flown by Captain Robert Harriger in company with Captain John Mainwaring in BW163. When the fighter was transferred to the 41st FS in late 1942 the previous 36th FS letter "H" was over-painted matt black as illustrated. This then served as a backdrop to the scoreboard and pilot names, and the squadron number 83 was applied to follow the last two digits of the British serial. This fighter was eventually scrapped at Amberley in 1944.

Profile 33: P-400 British serial AP294, 94, X, 30-Mile, January 1943

This P-400 was assigned to Lieutenant David Latane and had the Walt Disney cartoon characters of *Heckle & Jeckle* painted on the port and starboard doors. Latane bailed out of this P-400 north of 30-Mile 'drome on 9 February 1943 after it caught fire. It took him six days to make his way back to base after negotiating thick swamp.

Profile 34: P-400 British serial BW175, *Pat*, 175, Bankstown, April 1942

This Airacobra was diverted from Project X and arrived in Australia on 22 February 1942. It suffered an operational accident at Bankstown on an unknown date shortly thereafter which removed its starboard wing. Following extensive repairs, it was shipped to the Thirteenth Air Force in New Caledonia where it served with the 67th FS before it was condemned following another accident on 13 February 1943.

41st Fighter Squadron

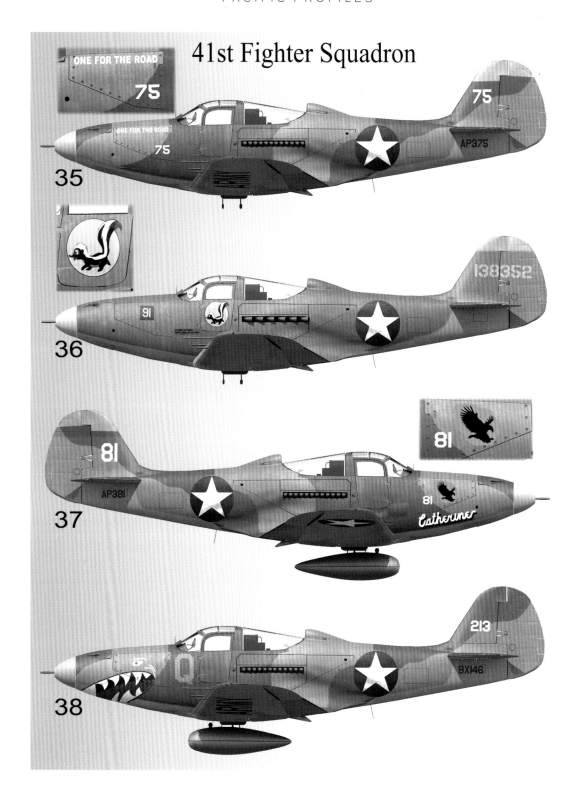

35

36

37

38

Profile 35: P-400 British serial AP375, *One for the Road*, 75, Bankstown, May 1942

This Airacobra was numbered from the last two digits in the British serial. Its combat history is unknown, however it was not lost to combat or operations.

Profile 36: P-39D-1 serial 41-38352, 91, Durand 'drome, February 1943

After serving with the 35th FS this Airacobra was transferred into the 41st FS and then back to the 35th FS around late 1942. On an unknown date in 1943 it had a landing accident at Durand 'drome (17-Mile) when flown by Lieutenant George Goolsby.

Profile 37: P-400 British serial AP381, *Catherine*, 81, Seven-Mile, July 1942

This P-400 entered service with the 41st FS in Australia on 15 April 1942 and then New Guinea where it was damaged during a Japanese air raid on an unknown date. It was later transferred to New Caledonia where it served with 67th FS, from which it was withdrawn from service on 25 November 1942.

Profile 38: P-400 British serial BX146, [batch 213], Q, Seven-Mile, August 1942

This Airacobra first served with the 80th FS which applied the shark teeth markings and assigned it the squadron letter "Q". After being transferred to the 41st FS it maintained the batch number 213 on the fin, using it as the *de facto* squadron number. On 1 September 1942 it crashed about a mile from Durand 'drome when Lieutenant George Helveston bailed out of the aircraft.

The ground crew of Profile 31, with "Tojo" Harries sitting on the wing.

41st Fighter Squadron

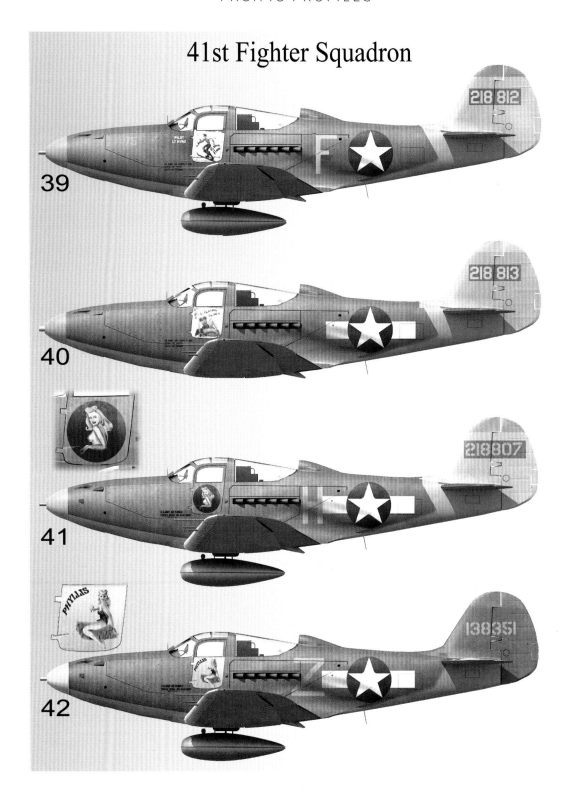

39

40

41

42

Profile 39: P-39N-5 serial 42-18812, *Flying Finn*, 75, F, Tsili Tsili, October 1943

Erick Kyro arrived in Port Moresby on 1 October 1942 and joined the 41st FS which was then based at Seven-Mile. His first Airacobra flight in the combat zone occurred on 15 October 1942, in his assigned P-400 named *Sisu*, and his last in this second assigned Airacobra, at Tsili Tsili on 28 November 1943. *Flying Finn*'s skier on the left door wore a Persian lamb black fur hat with a feather in it. A scarf flailed in the breeze, and the skier wore turned-up Finnish boots. *Flying Finn* is profiled as it appeared at Tsili Tsili in October 1943. It was transferred to the 110th RS(F) in January 1944 and was lost during a leaflet drop mission over Madang on 16 February 1944.

Profile 40: P-39N-5 serial 42-18813, *Blazing Blonde / Betty*, Tsili Tsili, August 1943

This P-39 was assigned into the 41st FS in August 1943 and named *Blazing Blonde* shortly thereafter by an unidentified pilot. It was subsequently transferred into the 110th RS(F) at the end of January 1944 when the squadron commenced transitioning to P-47Ds. It was lost with this unit on 6 July 1944 after it departed from Tadji flown by Lieutenant Gabriel Eggud. While making a low-level bomb run over Wewak, a bomb blast removed both wings and Eggud remains MIA. The Airacobra is illustrated as it appeared at Tsili Tsili in August 1943. After he received the fighter, Eggud painted the name *Betty* on the starboard engine panel.

Profile 41: P-39N-5 serial 42-18807, H, Tsili Tsili, August 1943

The aircraft was another N model assigned into the 41st FS in August 1943. It soon appeared with this door art although it was never named. The Airacobra is illustrated as it appeared at Tsili Tsili in August 1943. It ended its days being scrapped at Nadzab post-war.

Profile 42: P-39D-1 serial 41-38351, *Phyllis*, Z, Seven-Mile, April 1943

Assigned into the 41st FS in September 1942, this P-39 was named *Phyllis* with the door art as illustrated. It was assigned to a Lieutenant McCoy (first name unknown). It was one of two 41st FS Airacobras lost on 12 April 1943 during the Japanese Operation "I" raid against Port Moresby. Lieutenant Richard Culton was flying his 70th combat mission and was at 26,000 feet when he made a head-on attack against a Model 32 Zero whose return fire hit his engine and shot away his canopy. Culton's neck bled profusely through his leather helmet from shrapnel embedded in his scalp. A faltering engine saw him parachute near Haima village on the Brown River road where he took tea with surprised villagers before being returned to his airfield late that afternoon by a searching jeep. Culton was badly hurt from a hard parachute landing. The Zero attack had incurred head injuries which required long-term medical treatment. Unusually this Airacobra had a white spinner and is illustrated shortly after application of its door art.

Profile 37 after being damaged by a bomb blast at Port Moresby.

Profile 34 following its accident at Bankstown.

Profile 35 as it appeared at Bankstown where it first had its artwork applied.

Lieutenant Eric Kyro with Profile 39, the Flying Finn.

Profile 36 with its skunk door art.

41st FS Airacobra 42-18807, squadron letter H, is salvaged after a force-landing near Nadzab late 1943.

P-400 BW167 shortly after assembly at Tontouta in April 1942.

P-400 #35 of the 67th FS at Magenta, New Caledonia, following its collision with a USAAF Tiger Moth in December 1942.

CHAPTER 8
67th Fighter Squadron "Fighting Cocks"

The 67th FS is usually associated with the colourful shark-teeth P-400 Airacobras first involved in the gritty early Guadalcanal campaign. These were unpacked and assembled at Tontouta, New Caledonia, and the first of which was ready for a test flight on 28 March 1942. It was decided that the developed airfields extant on the island would be easy targets for air attack, so a series of four satellite fields was surveyed and used by the squadron's three flights. Flights of ten Airacobras dispersed to each field, with headquarters retained at Tontouta.

In April 1942 a pasture field near Noumea was first used, named Patsy after the callsign for its telephone exchange. "Patsy Flight" Airacobras soon appeared with the unique shark-teeth markings courtesy of pilot Lieutenant Peter Childress who modelled the design from a magazine photo he had of *Flying Tiger* P-40s in China. White Flight painted their spinners white, while Dumbea (modern-day Magenta Field northeast of Noumea) was home to Blue Flight which named itself "Pair-a-Dice" as a play on the word "Paradise", with blue spinners. Another field inland was nicknamed "Dustbowl" where Red Flight with red spinners made their home, painting the squadron motif "Fighting Cock" on the doors of the fighters.

Sometimes the flights also used another small grass airfield located near the township of Thio on the other side of island. This was nicknamed "Shoebox" due to its confined square shape, hemmed in by hills. Navigation exercises during this time included long-distance flights around the area to prepare for the move to Guadalcanal. These also permitted pilots to estimate fuel requirements and optimum engine settings for long distance flights. The 67th FS lost five P-400s to operational causes during its time on New Caledonia.

The first 67th FS detachment to enter combat departed Plaine des Gaiacs on 22 August 1942, and led by a B-17E, refuelled at Efate before proceeding to Espiritu Santo. The following morning they flew to Guadalcanal guided by two B-17Es, a second one trailing in case it had to drop a life raft to any downed pilot. This sector took just short of four hours and was flown at only 200 feet. The squadron fought its first combat at Guadalcanal on 24 August when two P-400s engaged *Ryujo* B5N2 Kates.

The 67th FS had its first combat loss on 30 August 1942 when two pilots were shot down, one of whom was captured and executed. In its first months of service the squadron flew a mixture of ground support and escort missions. By April 1943 it was routinely sharing pilots and aircraft with the 70th FS.

Then exceptionally, the 67th FS was transferred to Fifth Air Force command at Wards 'drome, Port Moresby, on 13 June 1943 where it was attached to the 36th FS to assist in escorting C-47 transports to Wau and Bulolo. During this time it used the callsign "Agate" but remained under Thirteenth Air Force administrative control while operating in conjunction with Fifth Air Force units. It also flew missions from Dododura and Gurney Field (Milne Bay) before taking up station on Woodlark Island when the airstrip there was completed on 15 July 1943. Sixteen of the squadron's Airacobras arrived on 23 July, making the 67th FS the first air unit to be permanently based at the field. At Woodlark the squadron conducted daily strafing training and radar tracking missions but saw nil action for the next few months, with a plummet in morale. The squadron history of the time notes that:

> … great percentage of enlisted personnel have been in the tropics 20 months and morale is low, with consistent nil results.

The final phase of the unit's Pacific deployment occurred in January 1944 when it moved to Green Island from Woodlark, with a rear echelon contingent remaining in the Russell Islands. Following the evacuation of Japanese airpower from Rabaul in February 1944 the unit's Airacobras commenced ground attack missions, experimenting with dive-bombing techniques and varied bomb loadings. Targets were widespread around New Britain, New Ireland and Bougainville. At Green Island the 67th FS conducted a tag-team effort with 68th and 70th FS Airacobras. Missions of up to two dozen Airacobras were a regular feature of this phase of the squadron's history, and Airacobra inventories were often mixed or swapped during this period. The 67th FS left the South Pacific when it moved to Noemfoor at the end of April 1944. During the nine months it was operational in New Guinea and then Woodlark Island the 67th FS lost 28 Airacobras, 16 to operations and 12 to combat.

Markings

The 67th FS exclusively operated P-400s until October 1942 when it received its first P-39K. The P-400s comprised 23 in the British serial BW108 to BW167 range, five in the BX range and five in the AP range, comprising the initial allotment of 33 airframes. When the squadron first set up on New Caledonia its three flights painted their spinners red, white or blue, and painted their wing tips white to facilitate visual alignment during formation flying. Squadron numbers were allocated as each airframe appeared in the inventory, either as a new aircraft or a replacement. Markings between these early P-400s often became mixed up when airframes were redistributed due to repairs or reassignments.

As replacement or new aircraft arrived they were allocated sequential numbers, sometimes replacing those lost. All P-400s were phased out of service by February 1943. The squadron had meanwhile started taking aboard P-39D, F and K models followed by the first N Models which arrived in June 1943, and finally Q models which appeared at the end of the year.

Towards the end of 1943 the Airacobras at Torokina started using a three-digit system whereby the units could be easily determined in the air; the first digit indicating the squadron to which the Airacobras was assigned: 200 series for the 12th FS, 300 series for the 70th FS and 400 series for the 68th FS. The 67th FS was not part of the system, however, and retained a two-digit numbering system for its entire Airacobra career.

Profile 43: P-400 British Serial BX239, *Lulu*, 18, (batch no. 480), Guadalcanal, January 1943

Unusually, this Airacobra retained several original RAF markings throughout its combat career including the batch number 480 stencilled on the fin. It remained in service on Guadalcanal until February 1943.

Profile 44: P-400 British serial unknown, 22, Dumbea, May 1942

This profile is a good example of the unique shark-teeth markings designed by pilot Lieutenant Peter Childress who modelled the design from a magazine photo of *Flying Tiger* P-40Bs in China. The teeth were applied using a stencil explaining the conformity of the design. This P-400 was transferred to Blue flight at some stage before serving at Guadalcanal.

67th Fighter Squadron

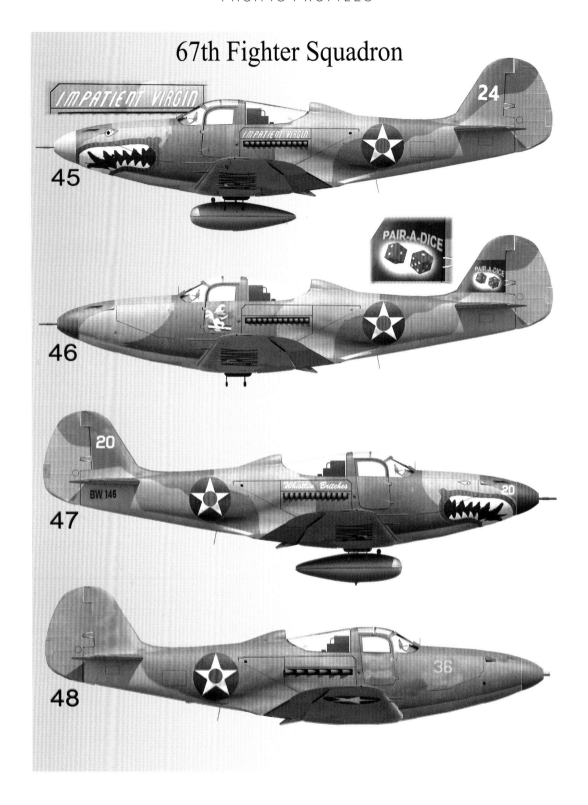

Profile 45: P-400 British serial unknown, *Impatient Virgin*, 24, Guadalcanal, August 1942

Another example of the Patsy Flight shark-teeth markings at "Patsy Field" shortly after the 67th FS took delivery of its Airacobras. This P-400 was among the first arrivals at Guadalcanal.

Profile 46: P-400 British serial unknown, *Pair-a-Dice* insignia, Guadalcanal, August 1942

The tail of this Airacobra was decorated at Dumbea airfield in April 1942, home to Blue Flight which named itself "Pair-a-Dice" as a play on the word "Paradise". This P-400 was also among the first arrivals at Guadalcanal where it appeared with a red spinner.

Profile 47: P-400 British serial BW146, *Whistlin' Britches*, 20, Guadalcanal, September 1942

Named after the whistling sound made on approach by the wind on its gun muzzles, this P-400 was written off on Guadalcanal on 24 November 1942 following an accident.

Profile 48: P-39D-1 serial unknown, 36, Espiritu Santo, December 1942

Illustrated as it appeared when being serviced with the 29th Air Service Depot at Espiritu Santo around December 1942, this P-39 was one of the earliest D models assigned into the 67th FS with no serial stencilled on the tail.

The subject of Profile 45 on New Caledonia in April 1942.

67th Fighter Squadron

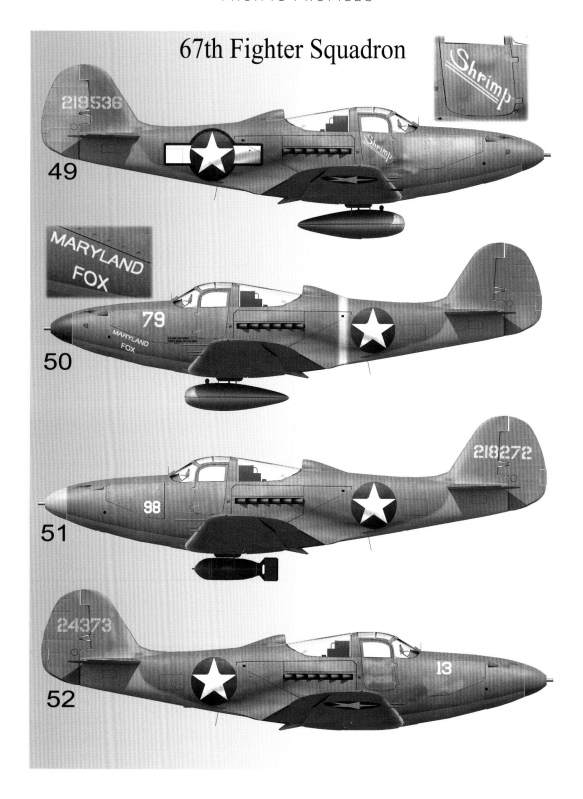

49

50

51

52

Profile 49: P-39N-5 serial 42-19536, *Shrimp*, Green Island, February 1944

This N model has an unusual history. In June 1943 it commenced service with the 72nd FS of the 318th FG whose task was the defence of Hawaii. It was one of a handful transferred to Australia from the Gilbert Islands in late 1943 where the 72nd FS later transitioned to P-38s. It is profiled as it appeared at Garbutt in early 1944 where it was overhauled. The light patch on the nose is where the previous 72nd FS squadron number was painted over. It then reassigned to the 67th FS at Green Island and allocated an unknown squadron number.

Profile 50: P-39N-5 serial unknown, *Maryland Fox*, 79, Ondonga, December 1943

This P-39 had a blue spinner and is profiled as it appeared at Ondonga in late 1943. It was regularly flown by Captain William Houseworth from the US state of Maryland. The white vertical fuselage band denotes Houseworth's status as a flight leader.

Profile 51: P-39N-1 serial 42-18272, 98, Munda, November 1943

This Airacobra is illustrated as it appeared at Munda in late 1943.

Profile 52: P-39K serial 42-4373, 13, Guadalcanal, May 1943

This Airacobra was filmed overhead Guadalcanal on 31 May 1943. It operated with the 67th FS for the remainder of the Pacific campaign.

67th FS P-39D-1 serial 41-38392 squadron number "31" parked at Tontouta around early 1943.

The 67th FS "Fighting Cock" motif applied to the door of a Red Flight Airacobra at "Dustbowl" airfield.

The subject of Profile 44, P-400 squadron number "22" parked at Dumbea around May 1942.

The subject of Profile 43 in a Guadalcanal revetment in January 1943. Note the RAF fin flash.

The first detachment of 67th FS Airacobras to arrive at Woodlark Island in late July 1943.

The subject of Profile 48 at the 29th Air Service Depot, Espiritu Santo.

The subject of Profile of 49, Shrimp, being serviced at Garbutt.

68ᵗʰ FS P-39Q Vivienne J at Torokina before it received a squadron number. The name Shaky is hand-painted above the exhaust stack.

CHAPTER 9
68th Fighter Squadron "Lightning Lancers"

The 68th FS arrived in Brisbane in early March 1942 then was briefly assigned to Amberley Field where the unit's engineers assembled P-400s and P-39Ds initially intended for them, however all were then transferred to the 8th FG. Instead, on 8 May the squadron sailed for Tongatabu equipped with 25 P-40Es in crates which they assembled and then flew patrols around the Tonga isles. On 2 November the squadron moved to Tontouta on New Caledonia where its pilots were attached to the 67th FS in whose Airacobras they started training while their P-40Es were all transferred to the RNZAF. However, the 68th FS was then re-equipped with P-40Fs (powered with Rolls-Royce Merlins) which they flew to Guadalcanal on Christmas Day 1942, setting up base at Fighter Two.

The 68th FS flew combat with their P-40Fs until converting to P-39s in June 1943 at Tontouta. They lost their first Airacobra to combat on 6 September 1943 when two went MIA during a dogfight with Zeros. In a similar way to the Airacobras of the 67th and 70th FS, detachments from the squadron also moved around the theatre, with Ondonga, Segi, the Russells and finally Torokina all being used as bases. The squadron took on the role of ground attack from late February 1944 onwards, using dive-bombing techniques with varied bomb loadings to attack targets in the New Britain/Bougainville area. Commanded by Major Leonard Shapiro, they moved to Torokina in April 1944 to undertake this task, conducting a tag-team effort with 67th FS and 70th FS Airacobras, often swapping pilots and aircraft. Missions of up to two dozen Airacobras were a regular feature of this phase of the squadron's history.

Bell Aircraft Corporation representative Earl Zelt, a civilian, assisted with technical advice on bomb loadings and delivery. The 68th FS's Airacobras left the South Pacific theatre from Torokina on 19 July 1944 aboard the SS *John Lykes* bound for Hollandia. In seven months of operating Airacobras in the South Pacific, the 68th FS lost a total of 11 to combat and two to operations.

Markings

The 68th FS first used a two-digit marking system, however towards the end of 1943 the Airacobras at Torokina started using a three-digit system whereby unit assignment could be more easily determined in the air. The first digit indicated the squadron to which the Airacobras were assigned: 200 series for the 12th Squadron, 300 series for the 70th FS and 400 series for the 68th FS.

68th Fighter Squadron

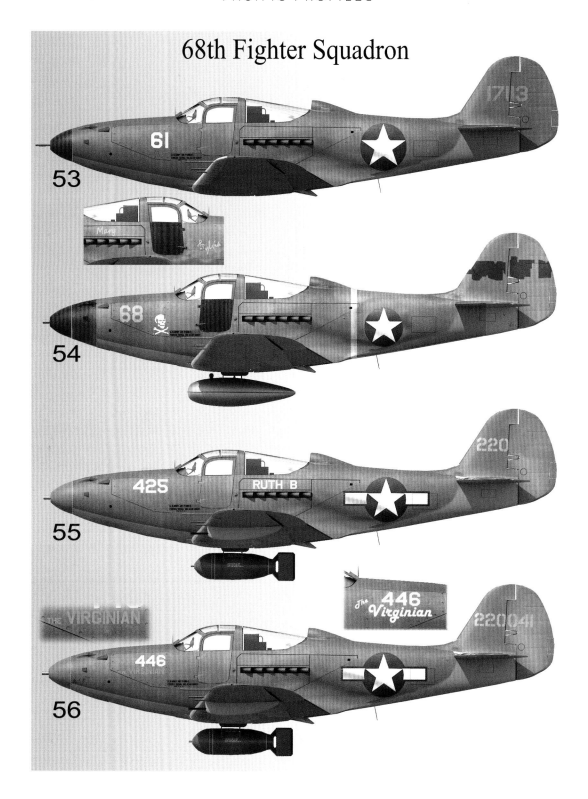

53

54

55

56

Profile 53: P-39D serial 41-7113, 61, Guadalcanal, June 1943

This P-39 was among several recycled 70th FS Airacobras issued to the 68th FS at Tontouta in June 1943 and was then operated by the squadron on Guadalcanal. Due to engine failure Lieutenant Thomas Clark ditched this fighter about 18 miles off Cape Esperance. This occurred during one of the squadron's first routine patrols from Fighter Two on Guadalcanal on the late afternoon of 5 July 1943. The sea was rough and although Clark was seen to get out, follow-up search missions the next day failed to locate him.

Profile 54: P-39K unknown serial, *Sylvia*, 68, Guadalcanal, circa May 1943

This P-39 was assigned to the only USAAF Airacobra ace, Lieutenant William Fiedler, who initially arrived in the theatre with the 70th FS. He first flew P-39D-1 "21" with the 70th FS and applied his hallmark skull and crossbones marking on the port side of the fuselage (see Profile 63). Fiedler was transferred to the 68th FS to assist with transition training and was assigned this recycled P-39K (often misidentified as a P-39N), on which he painted the forward nose and both doors red so he could be more easily recognised when airborne. The starboard side had the names *Sylvia* and *Mary*, the latter painted above the exhaust stack possibly by the crew chief.

The vertical fuselage band denoted his flight leader status and for unknown reasons the serial number was painted over. Fiedler had the identical skull & crossbones motif applied which he had used on his previous 70th FS mount. For unknown reasons the fuselage US insignia were reapplied in a smaller size than the factory markings, possibly as a result of past repairs. Fiedler chose the squadron number 68 for his mount but was killed on 30 June 1943 when the Airacobra he was flying that day was impacted by a departing P-38 at Guadalcanal.

Profile 55: P-39Q-5 unknown serial, *Ruth B*, 425, Ondonga, November 1943

This Airacobra was photographed departing Ondonga in late 1943 and was possibly P-39Q-5 42-20005 assigned to Major Leonard Shapiro, the 68th FS commander at the time.

Profile 56: P-39Q-5 serial 42-20041, *The Virginian*, 446, Ondonga, December 1943

This Airacobra was flown at Ondonga in late 1943 by Captain Tony Morrison.

Lieutenant William Fiedler's Profile 54 taxies at Guadalcanal.

The 68th FS taxies at Torokina, led by P-39Q 407.

The subject of Profile 55, P-39Q Ruth B, departs Ondonga.

Lieutenant William Feidler on the wing of the starboard side of Profile 54 at Fighter #2, showing the names Sylvia and Mary.

Lieutenant William Fiedler taxies the subject of Profile 63 at Nadi in late 1942.

CHAPTER 10
70th Fighter Squadron "White Knights"

The 70th Pursuit Squadron (later Fighter Squadron) operated Airacobras for more than two years before commencing transition to Lightnings in May 1944. It was the first USAAF unit based in Fiji, where it spent just over a year before being transferred to Guadalcanal. Their year in Fiji was sprinkled by a series of visits from US personalities and VIPs. Furthermore, the squadron boasted a celebrity amongst its ranks, being Sergeant Jack Dupree, the US Golden Gloves lightweight boxing champion, and undefeated US welterweight champion.

The 70th PS docked at Suva's main wharf at 1900 on 28 January 1942 aboard the USS *President Monroe*. The men were then transported to Nausori some 15 miles northwest where they were quartered in a sugar mill before transferring to nearby Nausori Airfield the next day, a grass strip recently built by RNZAF engineers.

Crated P-39D-1 Airacobras which had arrived with them as cargo aboard the USS *President Monroe* were floated in their crates up the Rewa River on barges, arriving on 5 February. These fighters were in the 41-7080 to 41-7115 serial range and four days later the first of these was assembled in time to conduct taxi trials. On 10 February Lieutenant Sharpsteen conducted the first flight in Fiji from Nausori.

It was decided to send a forward echelon to Nadi where there were better facilities, and on 13 February two P-39s flew there. On 17 February the final Airacobra was assembled at Nausori, rendering a total of 24 on charge. A Bell Aircraft civilian representative who had accompanied the squadron, Harold Lebonte, acted as advisor during assembly and testing of the fighters, much expediting progress.

In March, several US officers checked out in a RNZAF No. 4 Squadron Vickers Vincent stationed at Nausori, with the view to towing targets for aerial gunnery practice. The concept was abandoned when it became apparent that some of the rookie pilots were firing rounds too close for comfort. Rain was a constant problem at Nausori, causing more operational accidents. On 22 April, Lieutenants James Blose and Shaw launched on patrol, but weather closed in behind them. Blose disappeared, however the wreckage of his P-39 was discovered post-war in the mountains just inland from Nausori.

Combined manoeuvres were held at Nadi with 70th BS B-26s in July 1942. The 70th PS also acquired two L-2 Taylorcraft Grasshopper light aircraft for liaison purposes. These were mainly used to transport "brass" between Nadi and Nausori, however several trips included Suva, where enterprising pilots could land on the golf course, not far from RNZAF Headquarters at Laucala Bay.

The squadron's S-2 (Intelligence) officer was Thomas Lanphier, later to become a controversial Lightning pilot who participated in the Yamamoto mission. Another 16 Airacobras arrived in

The subject of Profile 57 written off at Nadi airfield on 27 February 1942. Note lack of serial number and the red circle in the national insignia.

The subject of Profile 60, Gypsy Rose Lee, parked under rain tress at Narewa, one of Nadi's airfields.

July, swelling its fighter ranks to more than three dozen. On 31 August 1942, the squadron was redesignated a "Fighter" squadron instead of "Pursuit".

On 11 January 1943, Second Lieutenant Arthur Debernarde bailed out of his P-39 when it stalled at 1,500 feet not far from Nadi. When he jumped, his pilot chute was severed when it struck the tailplane, resulting in Debernarde falling to his death. The following day the 70th FS celebrated the first anniversary of its departure from the US, however their recent attachment to the 347th Fighter Group meant they were about to enter combat. A few weeks later the squadron would be operational at Guadalcanal.

On 5 February 1943, the 70th FS flew seven P-39s direct from Nadi to Henderson Field, Guadalcanal, led by squadron commander Major Waldon Williams. This flight established a record for the longest P-39 delivery flight in the theatre to date. At Guadalcanal the pilots were attached to the 68th FS for two months to learn combat skills. One ground attack technique developed by the squadron during this time was dropping belly tanks on troop positions before strafing the contents with incendiaries to cause a fire.

For the next year the 70th FS mainly flew patrols and escorts, and sometimes fought Japanese fighters. Detachments moved around the theatre, with Ondonga, Segi, the Russell Islands and Torokina all being used as bases. When Japanese air power evacuated Rabaul in February 1944 the squadron's Airacobras took on the role of ground attack, experimenting with different bomb loadings and developing dive-bombing techniques to attack targets all over New Britain and Bougainville. They moved to Torokina to undertake this task, conducting a tag-team effort with 67th FS and 68th FS Airacobras. Bomb loadings included a single 1,000-pound bomb with 1/10 second fuse, two 250-pound demolition bombs under the wings or one 500-pound magnesium cluster bomb. Missions of up to two dozen Airacobras were a regular feature of this phase of the squadron's history. During this ground attack phase replacement civilian Bell Aircraft representative Earl Zelt assisted with technical advice. The squadron left Torokina for good on 2 May 1944 and moved to Ondonga where the pilots commenced transition to the P-38 Lightning.

Markings

None of the original batch of P-39D-1s assembled at Nausori had tail stencils. Most lay in the 41-7080 to 41-7115 serial range and were numbered consecutively as they were assembled, on the door commencing at 1. Several had nicknames painted on the tail. By the time the 70th FS reached Guadalcanal these numbers had moved forward of the door and appeared in smaller calligraphy. Many Airacobras had their spinners painted yellow, the squadron colour.

Towards the end of 1943 the Airacobras at Torokina started using a three-digit system whereby the units could be easily determined in the air. The first digit indicated the squadron to which the Airacobras were assigned: 200 series for the 12th FS, 300 series for the 70th FS and 400 series for the 68th FS.

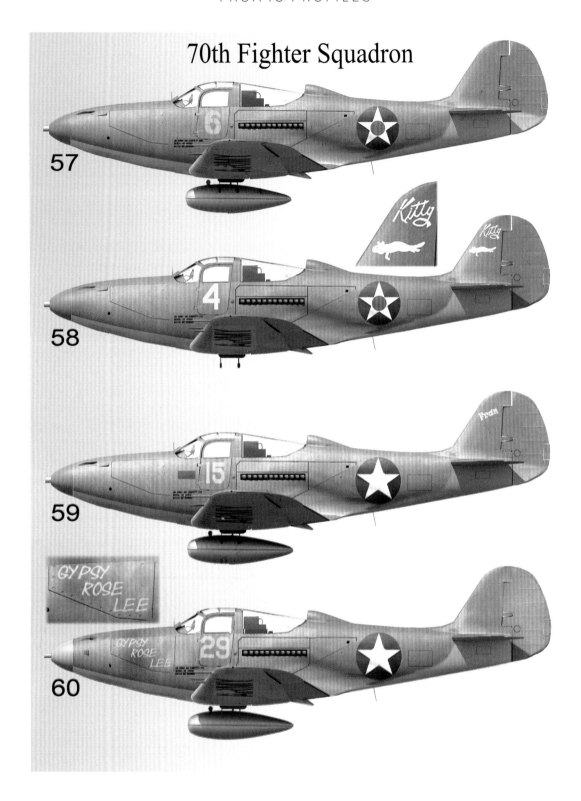

70th Fighter Squadron

57

58

59

60

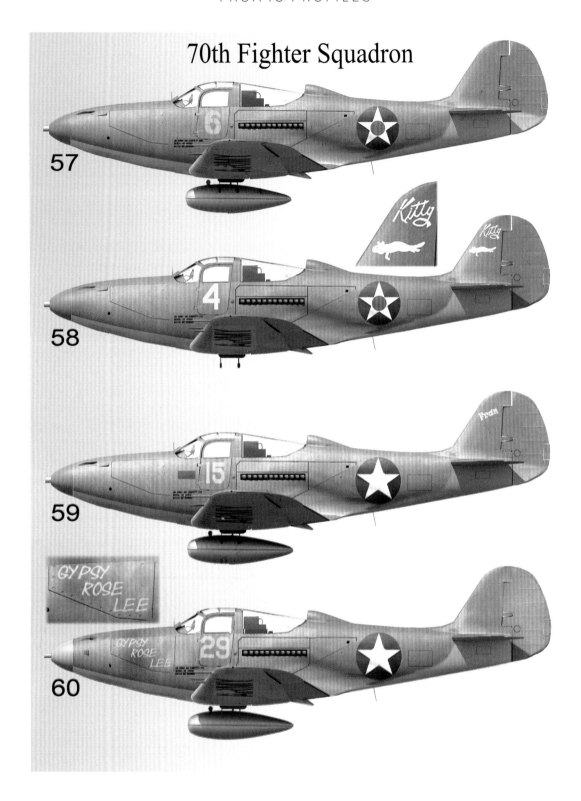

Profile 57: P-39D-1 serial 41-7106, 6, Nausori, February 1942

This Airacobra was among the first batch of P-39D-1s assembled at Nausori all of which lay in the 41-7080 to 41-7115 serial range, yet the serial was not stenciled on the fin. It is unclear how many were first assembled in this batch, but it was at least 15. All retained the early 1942 US insignia with red circle, and all had a consecutive squadron number applied as each was assembled. This P-39 was written off at Nadi airfield on 27 February 1942 during an operational accident.

Profile 58: P-39D-1 serial 41-7104, *Kitty*, 4, Nausori, April 1942

Named *Kitty* by Lieutenant James Blose, this Airacobra was named shortly after assembly at Nausori. Blose crashed in poor weather in the mountains behind Nausori on 22 April 1942 whilst returning from an exercise. The artwork on the fin is referenced from photos taken at the crash site.

Profile 59: P-39D-1 serial 41-7115, *Fran*, 15, Nausori, April 1942

This Airacobra was another from the first batch of P-39D-1s assembled at Nausori, photographed there at the end of April 1942 with the red circle painted over.

Profile 60: P-39D-1 serial unknown, *Gypsy Rose Lee*, 29, Narewa, January 1943

Photographed at Narewa near Nadi in early 1943, this P-39D-1 was among the second batch delivered to the 70th FS.

Pilot Captain Sidney Hardin (right) and his crew chief Sergeant Eddy with Fran, the subject of Profile 59.

70th Fighter Squadron

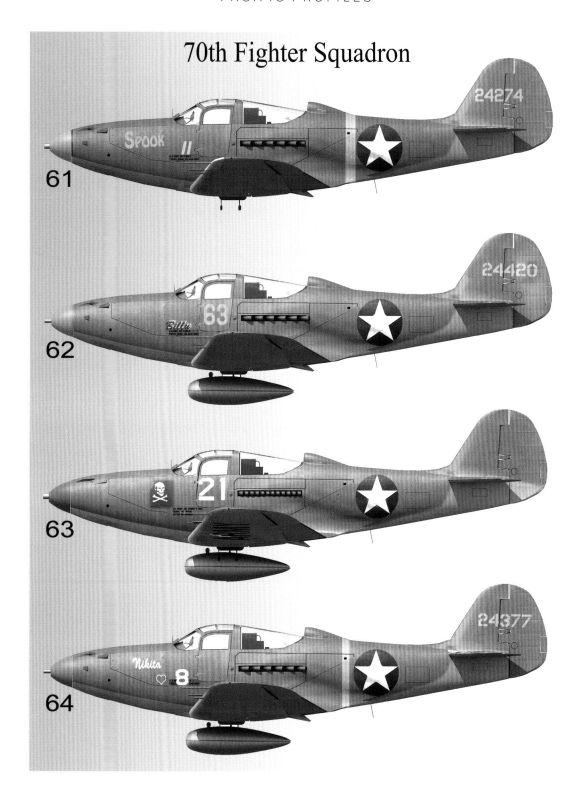

61

62

63

64

Profile 61: P-39K serial 42-4274, *Spook*, 11, Guadalcanal, March 1943

This K model was lost on 7 April 1943 when commanding officer Major Waldon Williams inexplicably dived away during a fighter interception and crashed into the ocean off Guadalcanal. The vertical fuselage stripe denotes his leadership status.

Profile 62: P-39K serial 42-4420, *Billy*, 63, Woodlark Island, July 1943

This K model served only briefly with the 70th FS before it was transferred into the 67th FS around March 1943. It was among the first batch of sixteen 67th FS Airacobras to arrive at Woodlark Island on 23 July 43, by which time it had been named *Billy*.

Profile 63: P-39D-1 unknown serial, 21, Narewa, May 1942

This P-39 was assigned to the only USAAF Airacobra ace, Lieutenant William Fiedler, who arrived in Fiji with the 70th FS. This was his first assigned P-39 to carry his hallmark skull and crossbones marking which was stenciled on both sides of the fuselage. Fiedler was later transferred to the 67th FS to assist with transition training where he was assigned a recycled P-39K (see Profile 54). The aircraft is profiled as it appeared at Narewa, Fiji, around May 1942.

Profile 64: P-39K serial 42-4377, *Nikita*, 8, Munda, November 1943

This K model replaced the first squadron number 8, a P-39D-1 lost in Fiji to unknown causes in 1942. *Nikita* was photographed at Munda in late 1943 where it was assigned to an unidentified flight leader.

The subject of Profile 65, Short Stroke, with its yellow spinner, often portrayed elsewhere wrongly with a blue one.

70th Fighter Squadron

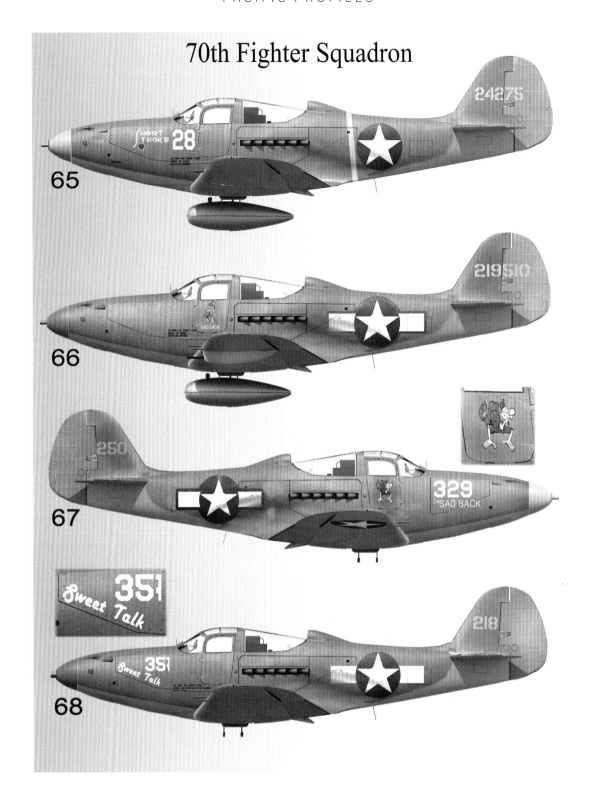

65

66

67

68

Profile 65: P-39K serial 42-4275, *Short Stroke*, 28, Guadalcanal, February 1943

This Airacobra flew all of 1943 with the 70th FS and was destroyed in an operational accident on 9 May 1944.

Profile 66: P-39N-5 serial 42-19510, *Sad Sack*, squadron number unknown, Torokina, November 1943

Illustrated as first assigned into the 70th FS with red surround insignia, this P-39 was assigned to Captain James Van Nada at Torokina, and later received an unknown squadron number.

Profile 67: P-39N-1 serial 42-18250, *The Sad Sack*, 329, Torokina, January 1944

This was the second *Sad Sack* named thus within the 70th FS, illustrated as it operated from Torokina in early 1944, fitted with a replacement rudder.

Profile 68: P-39N serial unknown, *Sweet Talk*, 351, Torokina, November 1943

This Airacobra was written off during an operational accident at Torokina in November 1943.

The subject of Profile 67 is in the foreground, with 12th FS P-39N Airacobra "249" next in formation. The photo exemplifies the degree to which, later in the war, missions were flown by pilots and aircraft from different Airacobra squadrons.

Engineers remove the gun panel of Profile 68, Sweet Talk, at Torokina while hunting for spares.

The subject of Profile 71 at Mareeba before its delivery flight to New Guinea.

Captain Phillip Rasmussen takes off in Profile 70, Sun Setter, from Milne Bay in September 1942.

CHAPTER 11
80th Fighter Squadron "Headhunters"

The 80th Pursuit Squadron disembarked at Brisbane from the USS *Maui* on 6 March 1942, alongside the other two squadrons of the 8th PG, the 35th and 36th PS. The 80th PS received both P-39Ds and P-400s assembled at Eagle Farm airport, before moving to Lowood airfield on 28 March. By 10 May the unit had relocated to Petrie airfield, just north of Brisbane, where it trained for about two months.

During this training phase they suffered several operational accidents. Lieutenant Maxwell Jones lost his life on 26 May when his P-400 hit a tree while landing at Petrie. Then on 2 July Lieutenant George Austin was killed when his P-39F collided with another P-39F while formation flying over Redcliffe, a coastal town not far to the east. On 15 July Lieutenant Travis Ferguson flew his P-400 too close to the water over Moreton Bay near Brisbane. The left wing clipped the water and the fighter fragmented when it hit at high speed. Later that same afternoon another P-400 aircraft flown by Lieutenant Joseph Cole inexplicably dove into Moreton Bay just off the northern Brisbane suburb of Sandgate.

The 80th FS moved to Port Moresby the following week on 20 July, then relocated to Milne Bay on 8 November. On 27 July after most of the squadron had moved to New Guinea, another operational takeoff accident claimed the life of Lieutenant Gilbert Oxley.

The 80th FS sent a small detachment of engineers to Australia to train on with P-38s in mid-October 1942 at Amberley. The squadron eventually took P-38s to New Guinea in March 1943, taking up station at 14-Mile 'drome. Most of their Airacobra inventory was transferred to the 41st FS, with a handful going to the RAAF.

The 80th FS's first combat loss occurred on 22 July only two days after the move to New Guinea when Lieutenant David Hunter was shot down near Japanese forces at Buna and later executed. The squadron lost eight Airacobras to training and operational accidents in Australia, and three in New Guinea. During its nine months of operating Airacobras in New Guinea it lost four to combat, with a combined total of nine fatalities from operational and combat losses. In New Guinea its Airacobras used the callsign "Copper".

Markings

Like its sister squadrons in the 8th FG, the 80th FS applied an alphabetical letter in white or yellow as the primary squadron identifier. The shark's teeth marking applied in white, black and red was a signature squadron marking, although this only appeared on the early P-400s.

80th Fighter Squadron

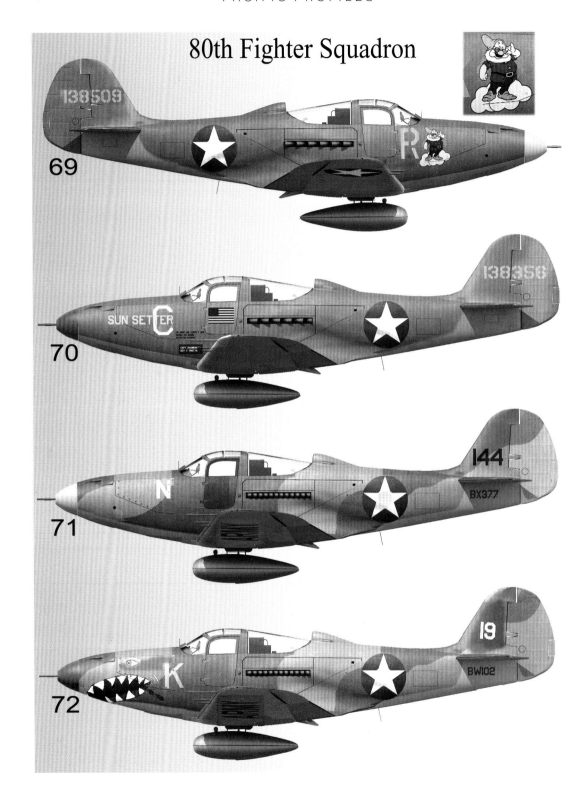

Profile 69: Bell P-39D-2 serial 41-38509, R, Milne Bay, November 1942

The Walt Disney dwarf was painted on the door of this P-39 when it was stationed at Milne Bay in November 1942. The fighter was reassigned to the 41st FS when its pilots moved to Australia to take up transition training to P-38s. Captain Albert Schinz from the 41st FS flew this P-400 on 12 April 1943 when he claimed a single-engine fighter over Port Moresby.

Profile 70: Bell P-39D-1, serial 41-38356, *Sun Setter*, C, Milne Bay, September 1942

Named by Captain Phillip Rasmussen, with crew chief Sergeant Tony Trotta, this Airacobra survived combat at Milne Bay. Rasmussen first painted the US flag on the door as illustrated here but later removed it as it contained too much red.

Profile 71: Bell P-400, British serial BX377, N, [batch no. 144], Port Moresby, July 1942

The wreckage of this Airacobra lies near the coast at Buna however the details of its loss are not clear. It is profiled just after it was first assigned into the 80th FS and allocated the letter N. The number 144 on the fin is the consignment batch number which was left there during the delivery flight to New Guinea.

Profile 72: Bell P-400, British serial BW102, 19, K, Port Moresby, August 1942

This P-400 first served with the 39th FS and was named *The Flaming Arrow* by Lieutenant Curran Jones (see Profile 22). Although the arrow nose art was painted over, the fighter retained most 39th FS markings including the blue spinner, tail tip and number 19 when it was transferred into the 80th FS at Port Moresby in late July 1942. The 80th FS gave it the squadron letter K and added the sharks teeth. This P-400 was eventually scrapped at Amberley.

Captain Phillip Rasmussen stands on the wing of Profile 70, Sun Setter, after the US flag was painted out.

80th Fighter Squadron

Profile 73: Bell P-400, British serial BW134, 37, M, Port Moresby, August 1942

This was another P-400 which retained its 39th FS markings including the number 37 when it was transferred into the 80th FS at Port Moresby in late July 1942. It was allocated the squadron letter M and had sharks teeth added. This P-400 was eventually scrapped at Amberley.

Profile 74: Bell P-39D-1 serial # 41-38352, D, Milne Bay, September 1942

The unique smirking Japanese skull motif painted on the port door was designed and applied by Lieutenant Leder at Milne Bay during the squadron's deployment there in August/September 1942. The design included a red bullet hole through the helmet and was influenced by a series of strafing missions against Japanese troop positions at Milne Bay in September 1942. Japanese helmets became collector's items after such missions. The narrow and square calligraphy of the letter "D" was unorthodox, and Leder's name was stenciled in white over a matt black square just below the serial block. This P-39 was scrapped in New Guinea after the war.

The subject of Profile 73 over Port Moresby.

Lieutenant Leder poses with Profile 74 at Milne Bay.

Pilot Lieutenant George Holt and Staff Sergeant Charles Chervank pose with Profile 75, Moise II, at Dobodura.

CHAPTER 12

82nd Reconnaissance Squadron (Fighter) "Strafin' Saints"

Two Fifth Air Force squadrons operated ground attack Airacobras in New Guinea: the 82nd RS(F) which arrived in New Guinea in October 1943 and the 110th RS (F) which docked at Brisbane on 5 December 1943 aboard the transport ship SS *Cape Mendocino*. Both squadrons were assigned to the 71st Tactical Reconnaissance Group, and by 17 December they had stationed themselves at Durand and Schwimmer 'dromes at Port Moresby to conduct familiarisation and in-country training. Pilots from both squadrons were initially attached to the 35th Fighter Group to acquire combat experience. On 26 December they departed the Port Moresby area and headed first to Dobodura. Later they would base themselves at Nadzab, Saidor, Finschhafen and Gusap.

From Dobodura the 82nd RS(F) flew bombing, strafing and low-level photo reconnaissance missions. Some Q models were field-modified with a fuselage camera, in addition to wing-mounted K-24 and/or K-25 cameras. Other field modifications included additional protection for the oil filter and glycol cooler. The *modus operandi* was to approach targets from behind hills for protection, whilst a cockpit intervalometer regulated camera shutters for photo-runs. Enemy shipping was a priority, and the aircraft's four 0.50-inch calibre machine guns and 20mm cannon were considered effective against these targets, particularly against Daihatsu supply barges, which were ubiquitous around New Guinea's northern shores.

In late January 1944 the 82nd RS(F) deployed to Gusap in the Ramu Valley, where its job was to support ground operations by Allied troops. Both RS(F) at this time each fielded about two dozen Airacobras in their inventories. Varying bomb loads used a mixture of 500-, 300-, 250- and 100-pound bombs mainly to attack troop positions. The squadron was renamed the 82nd Tactical Reconnaissance Squadron in July 1944.

Markings

By the time the 82nd RS(F) arrived in New Guinea the practice of painting white tails on Fifth Air Force fighters was commonplace. Sometimes the serial was reapplied over the tail, while on others the serial was masked off. For easy squadron identification a white band was painted around the nose which completely circumnavigated the fuselage. This was of varying width but generally between three to four inches wide. Nearly every Airacobra carried a nickname, and crew chiefs also had their say on the engine cowling usually above the exhaust stack. All 82nd RS(F) Airacobras had a white spinner.

82nd Reconnaissance Squadron (Fighter)

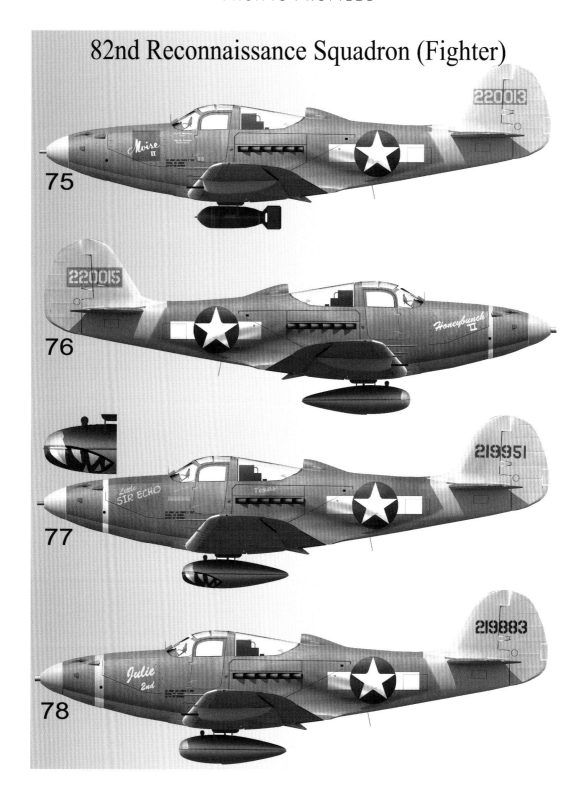

Profile 75: Bell P-39Q-5 serial 42-20013, *Moise II*, Gusap, January 1944

This Q model was first assigned into the 36th FS and allocated the squadron letter M before reassignment to the 82nd RS(F) in December 1943 where it was painted over. Around early November 1943 the serial number was masked off and the tail painted white in accordance with the Fifth Air Force IFF requirements. *Moise II* was assigned to Lieutenant George Holt but was destroyed in an operational accident on an unknown date. It was replaced by another Q model Airacobra which Holt named *Moise 3rd*.

Profile 76: Bell P-39Q-5 serial 42-20015, *Honeybunch II*, Saidor, May 1944

The original *Honeybunch* was an N model Airacobra flown by squadron commander Major Donald Gordon in the US prior to reassignment to New Guinea. Gordon flew *Honeybunch II* until 4 June 1944 when it was impacted by a departing P-47D which suffered a blown maingear tyre, destroying both aircraft.

Profile 77: Bell P-39Q-5 serial 42-19951, *Little Sir Echo*, Nadzab, June 1944

This P-39Q was often flown by Captain Lyndall Tate from Texas and named after "Echo" the nickname for his wife. Tate's sense of humour saw him paint a shark-mouth on several of his drop tanks. He returned home in November 1944 after a year's combat, but stayed on as a pilot after the United States Air Force was formed in 1947. He continued to fly for the next three decades and his service included one tour of Vietnam. Tate passed away in 2008.

Profile 78: Bell P-39Q-5 serial 42-19883, *Julie 2nd*, Finschhafen, February 1944

This Airacobra served the 82nd RS(F) until September 1944, when its entire inventory of Airacobras was retired for overhaul due to high airframe hours. They traded their P-39Qs for P-40Ns, and the overhauled Airacobras were then transferred to the 110th RS(F) including *Julie 2nd*. Since the 110th RS(F) was still operating Airacobras, it took the pick of the bunch leaving most 82nd RS(F) Airacobras to be abandoned on the side of Tadji field. These were cannibalised for parts to keep the remaining 110th RS(F) Airacobras airworthy. *Julie 2nd* was struck off charge in May 1945 but is profiled as it appeared as a new aircraft with the 82nd RS(F) at Finschhafen, in February 1944, complete with a new black stencil serial number applied over a freshly painted white tail.

Unidentified P-39Q Ha-ard Luck at Dobodura with its crew (left to right) armourer Corporal Salwyn, pilot Lieutenant Pictor and crew chief Staff Sergeant Egoff.

Profile 77, Little Sir Echo, with one of its shark-teeth drop tanks at Finschhafen. P-39Q Ruthie II is to the far left of the photo.

Commanding officer Major Donald Gordon poses with Profile 76, Honeybunch II, at Dobodura. The armourer for this Airacobra was Corporal Robert Saint and the crew chief was Staff Sergeant Cecil Durden.

P-39N 42-18404 was named My Wild Irish Rose and is seen here undergoing maintenance at Dobodura in February 1944.

Profile 79, Pee Wee, receives an engine change at Tadji. Note the RAAF Beauforts in the background.

CHAPTER 13

110th Reconnaissance Squadron (Fighter) "Musketeers"

As described in the previous chapter, the 82nd RS(F) and the 110th RS(F) docked at Brisbane on 5 December 1943 aboard the transport ship SS *Cape Mendocino*. Forming the 71st Reconnaissance Group, the two squadrons were temporarily assigned to the 35th Fighter Group at Durand and Schwimmer 'dromes near Port Moresby to conduct familiarisation and in-country training.

On 26 December the 110th RS(F) covered the capture of Cape Gloucester before on 3 January 1944 covering the Saidor landing. On 20 January an advance detachment of nine 110th RS(F) P-39Qs was sent to Gusap, accompanied by more Airacobras from the 82nd RS(F). Their job from Gusap was to support ground operations by Allied troops. Both squadrons at this time each fielded about two dozen Airacobras in their inventories.

The 110th RS(F) later moved to Tadji in June 1944 where they stayed for three months participating in the mopping up of Japanese forces around the Wewak area, working alongside No. 100 Squadron, RAAF, Beauforts. Strafing and bombing missions of up to a dozen Airacobras were a common occurrence. Varying loads saw a mixture of 500-, 300-, 250- and 100-pound bombs used mainly to attack troop and gun positions. These were the last Airacobra missions flown in New Guinea after which both RS(F) moved to Biak towards the end of the year. There the 110th RS(F) was redesignated the 110th Tactical Reconnaissance Squadron in July 1944.

Markings

Like their 82nd RS(F) counterparts, most of the squadron's Airacobras had white spinners, with limited exceptions, however they lacked the white band on the forward fuselage. Instead, they painted their tail tips yellow. Each aircraft was allocated a squadron number between 10 to 40, applied in large digits using a unique calligraphy. While most numerals were painted in white a small number also appeared in yellow. Some digits had narrow black piping to accentuate the number's visibility. Many Airacobras applied door art and nicknames.

110th Reconnaissance Squadron (Fighter)

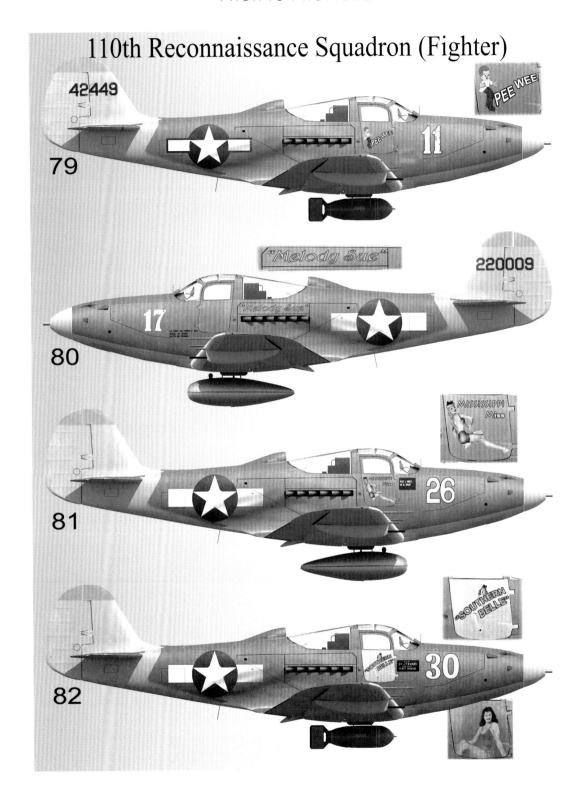

79

80

81

82

Profile 79: Bell P-39Q-20 serial 44-2449, *Pee Wee*, 11, Tadji, July 1944

This late model Airacobra was named and often flown by Lieutenant George Schultz, leader of B Flight at Tadji. *Pee Wee* was Schultz' nickname and the painted nose art only appeared on the starboard door alongside this cartoon character.

Profile 80: Bell P-39Q-5 serial 42-20009, *Melody Sue*, 17, Gusap, April 1944

The top engine cowl was easily removed, making this panel easy to decorate.

Profile 81: Bell P-39Q serial unknown, *Mississippi Miss*, 26, Gusap, May 1944

This Airacobra was assigned to Lieutenant Grover Denlinger, later killed in action in the Philippines on 15 December 1944.

Profile 82: Bell P-39Q serial unknown, *Southern Belle*, 30, Gusap, May 1944

Often flown by Lieutenant JT Evans and Lieutenant Thomas, this Airacobra later had the name *Julie* painted in Times Roman script on the exhaust access panel. The original door art appears in the lower panel.

Lieutenant JT Evans standing on the wing of Profile 82, at Gusap. The artwork is the original door art shown in the lower panel of Profile 82.

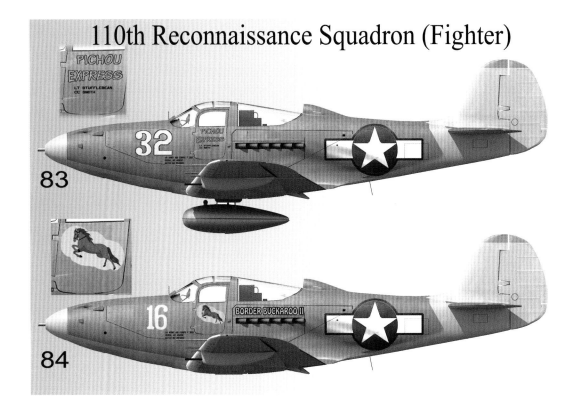

110th Reconnaissance Squadron (Fighter)

Profile 83: Bell P-39Q serial unknown, *Pichou Express*, 32, Tadji, September 1944

This Airacobra was named and often flown by Lieutenant Denver Stufflebean.

Profile 84: Bell P-39Q serial unknown, *Border Buckaroo II*, 16, Tadji, September 1944

This fighter was named by Lieutenant DeVore (first name unknown). The 110th TRS was originally a National Guard unit from Missouri, explaining the cowboy themes of its art.

Profile 80, Melody Sue, at Tadji, with an L-5 of the 25th Liaison Squadron in the background.

Framed by a P-40N spinner, squadron number "40" was 110th RS(F) P-39N-5 serial 42-19016 seen here at Gusap.

Unique Airacobras

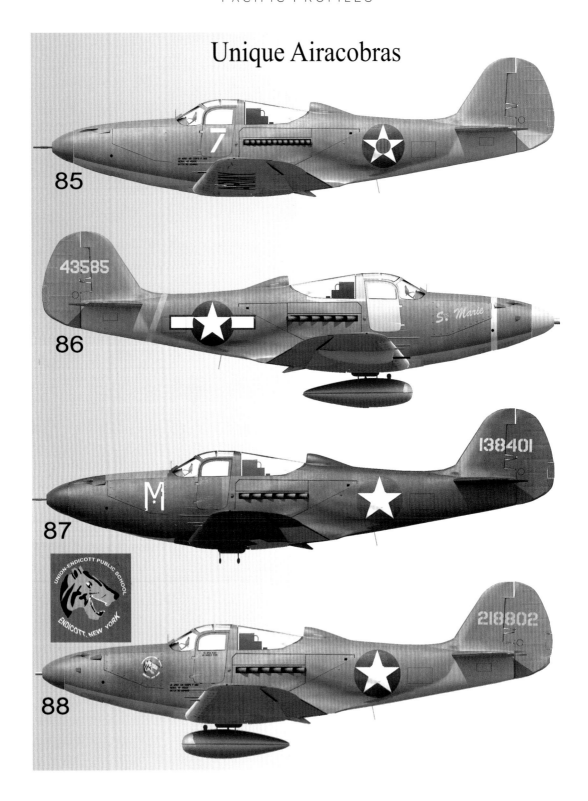

CHAPTER 14
Unique Airacobras

Profiles 85 to 92 illustrate Airacobras which had a unique history of markings as discussed below. Profiles 93 to 96 illustrate the changing markings on one particular P-400 Airacobra which showcases how markings could be varied as an Airacobra was transferred between units.

Profile 85 – first Airacobra lost in the Pacific
P-39D serial 41-7107, 7, 70th PS, Narewa detachment (Nadi), February 1942

This was the first Airacobra lost in the Pacific, unusually flown by a RNZAF pilot, Flight Lieutenant Eric Griffiths. Griffiths had a colourful history, having worked in China as a pilot in the early 1930s before joining US Admiral Richard Byrd's 1934/35 Antarctic Expedition. He subsequently joined the International Squadron of the Spanish Republican Air Force, flying Nieuport D.52 and Dewoitine D.372 biplanes. Griffiths was employed under a mercenary contract and was wounded in combat, for which he was compensated £1,000.

After failing in an attempt to raise a volunteer air arm in Ethiopia, Griffiths returned to New Zealand in 1937 and joined the RNZAF. By 1942 he had been posted to Fiji with No. 4 Squadron operating Vincents, where he was appointed RNZAF Liaison Officer to the USAAF.

On 23 February 1942, Griffiths was flying 41-7107 and made a mock gunnery pass against a Vincent. During a steep turning climb the Airacobra suddenly spun and crashed five miles southeast of Nadi airfield. Griffiths was killed and is buried in Suva's Commonwealth War Cemetery overlooking the harbour.

Profile 86 – last Airacobra lost in the Pacific
P-39Q-20 serial 44-3585, *Ste. Marie*, 71st TRS, crashed 25 September 1944

Named *Ste. Marie* (Ste. being the abbreviation for the French word "Sainte"), this P-39 was the last lost to combat in the Pacific. On 25 September 1944 Major Jack Prindeville was at cruise altitude when his engine caught fire. He bailed out however his parachute failed to open. The yellow oblique fuselage stripe indicates squadron leader status.

Profile 87 – Airacobra night fighter
P-39D-1 serial 41-38401, M, 35th FS

This P-39 was assembled at Amberley circa August 1942 and was one of 96 P-39Ds delivered to Australia just before P-39K/Ns started arriving a month later. Major Norman "Coach" Morris commanded the 35th FS from October 1942 to March 1943. The uncommon all black livery of this aircraft hails from an experimental night fighter scheme trialled by Morris following the

Unique Airacobras

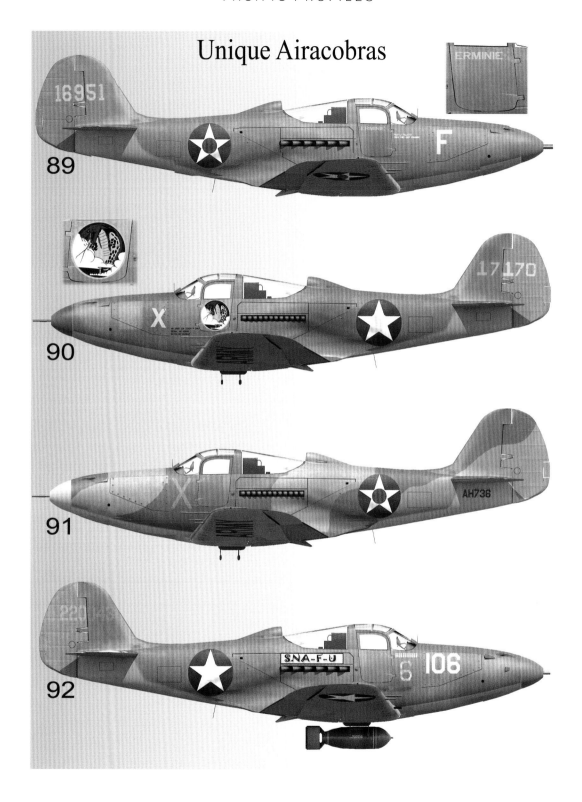

89

90

91

92

July 1942 night raids against Townsville by Emily flying boats. Morris identified his Airacobra with the letter "M", which was also the first letter of not only his surname, but also his rank and the surname of his mechanic, Staff Sergeant Matteo. On 24 March 1943 pilot Paul Beaubien was killed when this aircraft crashed into the ocean to the north of Cairns.

Profile 88 – Public donation fighter
P-39N-5 serial 42-18802, 41ˢᵗ FS, late July 1943

This Airacobra is illustrated as it was delivered to the 41ˢᵗ FS at Port Moresby. The aircraft was donated by funds raised by the Union Endicott Public School in New York. The tiger is the insignia of the school, and is still used today.

Profile 89 – the last survivor
P-39F-1 serial 41-6951, *Erminie*, F, 36ᵗʰ FS

This P-39 was the first Airacobra to land in New Guinea on 5 April 1942. Flown by Lieutenant Charles Faletta it was part of an advance 36ᵗʰ FS detachment sent to gain combat experience. It was later one of six which left Antil Plains for a delivery flight to Port Moresby on 1 May 1942. However, they got lost after encountering an intense storm near Horn Island. Faletta finally force-landed this Airacobra wheels-down, along with the other five which also put down. Faletta was eventually rescued, and his Airacobra was recovered in 1972. It was displayed at the Military Aviation Museum near Mareeba for many years. It is the only surviving Airacobra from the first batch delivered to Australia.

Profile 90 – assigned to Fifth Fighter Command
P-39F-1 serial 41-7170, X, 35ᵗʰ FS

This P-39 was one of the Project X deliveries assembled in Australia in April 1942. It was flown by Lieutenant Colonel Boyd "Buzz" Wagner on the first Airacobra mission in New Guinea against Lae and Salamaua on 30 April 1942. It was written off during an operational accident at Port Moresby on 1 July 1943 in unknown circumstances. This P-39 was one of many which had the 39ᵗʰ FS insignia painted on the door soon after being assembled, although Wagner was assigned to Fifth Fighter Command for the mission. As explained in Chapter 9, the 39ᵗʰ FS was ordered to remove all cobra squadron insignia a few weeks later on security grounds.

Profile 91 – British Ocean Green/grey colour scheme
P-400 serial BW AH736, X, 35ᵗʰ FS

This P-400 plus AH728 were both assembled at Amberley in March 1942. They were the only two Airacobras to be delivered to the Pacific theatre in the British Ocean Green and grey colour scheme which pertained to all Airacobras in the AH series. AH736 served briefly with the 35ᵗʰ FS as illustrated here before serving with the 80ᵗʰ FS.

Profile 92 – The 100 series
P-39Q-5 serial 4220043, *SNAFU*, 106, 44th or 339th FS

Sometime between mid to late 1943 all Thirteenth Air Force Airacobra squadrons commenced using a three-digit numbering system so that units could be more easily determined in the air; the first digit indicated the squadron to which the Airacobras was assigned: 200 series for the 12th FS, 300 series for the 70th FS and 400 series for the 68th FS. This was a rare case of a 100 series aircraft.

It appears likely this aircraft was assigned to the 44th and 339th Fighter Squadrons which briefly operated Airacobras, however this was never formalised as such. An advance detachment of seven 339th FS pilots was sent to Guadalcanal in September 1942. Having not received their promised Lightnings, they flew 67th FS Airacobras in combat during October-November 1942.

Later, between July and December 1943, a handful of 339th FS pilots again flew Airacobra missions with 67th and 68th FS aircraft, as they had more pilots than Lightnings. The 44th FS also briefly used the Airacobra for around ten weeks between September and October 1943 when it relinquished its previous P-40 inventory, and before it could take delivery of P-38s. It is likely that this Airacobra was flown by either the 44th or 339th FS in this late 1943 timeframe.

With a bomb slung under each wing, the subject of Profile 86 departs Biak. Note the replacement unpainted aluminium door.

Major Norman "Coach" Morris at Milne Bay with the subject of Profile 87.

P-39Ns numbered in the 100s series fly over the northern Solomons in late 1943.

The subject of Profile 92 at Torokina with a 500-pound bomb slung under the fuselage.

A Cobra's Four Lives

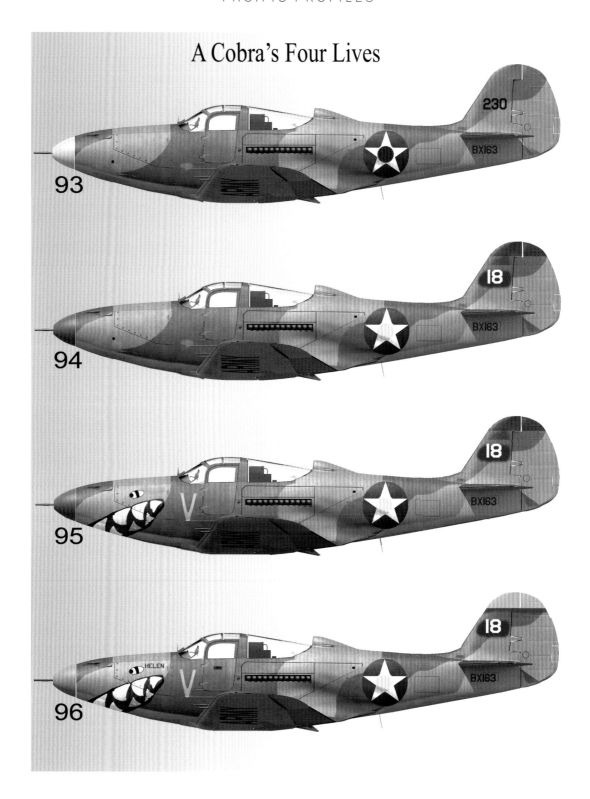

93

94

95

96

Profiles 93 to 96 – Markings in Transition
Bell P-400 British serial BX 163 *Helen*, 18, 39th, 80th & 36th FS

These four profiles outline the markings history of a P-400 Airacobra delivered and assembled in Australia in early 1942, and underline the degree to which markings were carried through to other units. Profile 93 showcases the markings when it was assembled and delivered in February 1942, still with the black consignment stencil 230 on the tail. In Profile 94 it carries the blue spinner and tail tip of the 39th FS. The batch number has been painted over and replaced by squadron number 18. Then, in late July 1942 the aircraft was transferred to the 80th FS in Profile 95 and shark's teeth were added. As seen in Profile 96, by December 1942 it continued to serve as "V" with the 36th FS which had repainted the spinner and tail tip yellow, and added the name "Helen". The unknown pilot's name was also stenciled on the door.

The aircraft had an operational accident on 24 December 1942 at Schwimmer 'drome. Although it was subsequently repaired and returned to service, little else is known of this fighter's subsequent history.

The subject of Profile 96 after its operational accident of 24 December 1942 at Schwimmer 'drome, Port Moresby.

End of the road for P-400s and P-39Ds which have done their time in combat, Amberley RAAF base, early 1944.

P-39D 41-38484 Daisy Mae when used as a 12th FS hack in 1944 (see also Profile 6).

Sources & Acknowledgments

Research for this volume draws exclusively from primary sources. The author's extensive collection of photos and notes from field trips contains much information obtained over many years for which it is not practicable to further credit, other than the sources listed below.

Thanks to website www.pacificwrecks.com and its hard-working owner, Justin Taylan.

Special thanks to the Fiji villagers who led the author to the wreck of P-39D 41-7104 in the hills behind Nausori in 1996.

Allied Air Force Intelligence Summaries (AWM)

Allied Translator and Interpreter Section (ATIS) Reports

ANGAU patrol officer reports of Allied crash sites, 1940s-1970s

Bell Aircraft Corporation Historical Records

Cairns Historical Society

Diary of Jack Fox, Courtesy North American Aircraft Corporation

Horn Island Museum photos via Vanessa Crowdey

Airacobra markings details from Individual Deceased Personnel Files

MacArthur Archives, MacArthur Memorial, Norfolk, VA

Field records and notes of Bill Chapman, Former Chemist in Port Moresby in the 1960s

Numerous Field Trips by the author To New Guinea and the Pacific, 1964-2017

Pacific Aircraft Historical Society - Wreck Data Sheets

Papua New Guinea Colonial Office - Civil Administration Records

Papua New Guinea Cultural Museum

Records and photos, Bruce Hoy, Former Curator of PNG Cultural Museum

RAAF Museum - Log Book Entries, Townsville Control Tower April 1942

USAAF Historical Study #17 - Air Action in the Papuan Campaign

Field notes of Robert Greinert, Airacobra wreck sites, PNG, 2011-2018

Newspaper 'The Courier Mail', microfilms held in Brisbane, Australia

Newspaper 'The Courier Post' (PNG), articles from past editions 1970s

Recollections and Records of Airacobra pilots Roy Seher, Charlie King, Don McGee

Papua New Guinea Catholic Mission Association

Records and Field Trips of John Douglas, Papua New Guinea, and made with James Luk, PNG 1976

Microfilms/ official records

Fifth and Thirteenth AF Units via Maxwell AFB: 5th Air Force Establishment, 8th FG, 35th FG, 36th FS, 80th FS, 110th TRS, 4th Air Depot, 27th Air Depot, 12th FS, 36th FS, 39th FS, 40th FS, 41st FS, 67th FS, 68th FS, 70th FS, 82nd TRS.

Index of Names